THE ARCHITECTS' ARCHITECT

BELLEW PUBLISHING CHARLES RENNIE MACKINTOSH SOCIETY

MURRAY GRIGOR

RICHARD MURPHY

THE ARCHITECTS' ARCHITECT: CHARLES RENNIE MACKINTOSH

First published in Great Britain in 1993
by Bellew Publishing Company Limited
in association with the Charles Rennie Mackintosh
Society

Bellew Publishing Company Limited
8 Balham Hill, London SW12 9EA

Origination and Manufacture by
Excel Graphic Press, Hong Kong
Typesetting Goodfellow & Egan, Cambridge

Designed by Ray Carpenter

ISBN 1 85725 043 5

The Charles Rennie Mackintosh Society is an award winner under the Business Sponsorship Incentive Scheme for its support of *The Architects' Architect: Charles Rennie Mackintosh*. The BSIS is a Government Scheme administered by the Association for Business Sponsorship of the Arts.

CONTENTS

INTRODUCTION

In recognition of Glasgow's year as European City of Culture 1990, Bishop and Robertson Chalmers sponsored the highly successful exhibition, 'Contemporary Visions', which featured installations from some of the world's leading architects and designers, paying homage to the continuing influence of Mackintosh, appropriately housed in the Glasgow School of Art.

As solicitors, a lot of our work is property-related and in such a prestigious city as Glasgow, architecture is always an important issue.

In their own architecture, contemporary architects of international influence such as Hans Hollein, Aldo van Eyck and Arata Isosaki have come to appreciate how Mackintosh fused the seemingly divergent influences of his own Scottish building heritage with foreign traditions into a synthesis that was at once modern, of its place and all his own.

Our support of this exhibition was recognized through an award from the Association of Business Sponsorship of the Arts (ABSA), an independent private-sector organization, on behalf of the Minister for the Arts.

Bishop and Robertson Chalmers are delighted to use the financial award to provide further support, through the publication of this commemorative book, which will serve to encourage an even greater awareness of the continuing influence and impact of this important Scottish architect, artist and designer.

BISHOP
AND
ROBERTSON
CHALMERS
SOLICITORS

GLASGOW & EDINBURGH

No. 4 Blythswood Square, Glasgow where Mackintosh is believed to have designed The Glasgow School of Art. The office now houses one of Scotland's leading law firms Bishop and Robertson Chalmers.

PREFACE

'Aspects of Genius (Mackintosh and his relevance today)' was the title of a major international conference organized by the Charles Rennie Mackintosh Society in association with the Glasgow School of Art in August 1990, as their contribution to Glasgow's year as European City of Culture.

Two exhibitions complemented this Mackintosh 1990 conference, both mounted at the Glasgow School of Art. One, 'Mackintosh in Context', highlighted architects and designers who, at the beginning of the twentieth century, were seen to draw inspiration from Mackintosh's own work. It is the other, 'Contemporary Visions', which this book celebrates.

Over 150 delegates attended the conference, to be addressed by speakers from many parts of the world, but on the Friday morning architects who had contributed to 'Contemporary Visions' took part in a session entitled 'Mackintosh as a Contemporary Force'. This event, the full background of which is given elsewhere, was an outstanding success, stimulating considerable press and television coverage.

There were many generous sponsors for the events, but the Charles Rennie Mackintosh Society is particularly indebted to Bishop and Robertson Chalmers, Solicitors, who sponsored the exhibition 'Contemporary Visions' which, with further funding from Glasgow District Council's Festivals Budget, attracted several of the world's leading architects to Glasgow and provided an opportunity for students of the Glasgow School of Art to work closely with these designers of international renown. This made it possible for the Society to apply for a BSIS award, which in turn has enabled this book to be produced.

A publication such as this, with contributions from internationally known architects with vigorously held views, will inevitably arouse controversy.

Thus it must be stated that the opinions expressed are those of the authors. Neither the Society nor the Glasgow School of Art can be held responsible for them. We hope and expect they will provoke discussion. We also hope that the observations made will help to encourage a greater awareness of the importance of Mackintosh in the world of architecture and design today.

Thanks are due to Murray Grigor, who originated the idea of the 'Contemporary Visions' exhibition, and to Richard Murphy, who managed the production. Both have contributed to this book. Thanks must also be given to the Glasgow School of Art for allowing such interventions in the fabric and space of Mackintosh's building and, of course, to the architects concerned who gave of their time and expertise.

A final note of appreciation must also be expressed to all those who participated in Mackintosh 1990, whether as sponsors, lecturers or delegates, and last but not least to our patient publishers and printers.

Patricia Douglas
Director, Charles Rennie Mackintosh Society

'Charles Rennie Mackintosh' by Francis Newbery. Oil 110.5 × 614 cm, *c.*1914. Scottish National Portrait Gallery.

FOREWORD MURRAY GRIGOR

The Austrian architect, Josef Hoffmann, wrote this assessment of his contemporary and friend Charles Rennie Mackintosh in 1929, the year after Mackintosh died:

> Ruskin and Morris both sought to awaken humanity to the beauty of good craftmanship and genuine material, and gradually introduced old techniques and methods of work. Ashbee, in 1885, went farther and produced in the Guild of Handcraft [*sic*] excellent modern silver work – although again in antique form. The development of the art of the Scot Mackintosh into a wholly new, original style is amazing. His rooms in pale grey wood and violet struts and embroidery adorned with rose-red flowers, his original lighting and glass, his heating apparatus, indeed every detail, were remarkable and full of promise. Innumerable forces bestirred themselves, seeking to evoke, in England [*sic*] first, then in Holland, Germany, Austria, France and the Scandinavian countries, a great, genuine, and creative artistic movement, to help the world to reach again a unity of culture.

Requoted in *Encyclopaedia Britannica*
'Interior Decoration, Modern'; 14th edition, 1929

Significantly, this assessment of Mackintosh's achievement in the round was written by an architect. What would architects say about Mackintosh today?

> With architecture way down in the dumps
> there is no better 'school' for us all.

This was how the Dutch architect, Aldo van Eyck, greeted summer visitors to the Glasgow School of Art. On his green latticed stand, placed in the gallery to confront the corridor fire doors (which Glasgow School of Art had installed in the 1960s), there were other more controversial statements. 'Retrieve what was lost . . . Remove those fire doors!' ran the headlines above sepia photographs which showed that in Mackintosh's original plan the stairwell and gallery space flowed unimpededly into the corridors as indoor streets.

This wonderful provocation was one of six installations created by internationally known architects around the School of Art in August 1990 with the aim of celebrating Mackintosh as an *architects' architect*. The idea was to highlight the architecture of Mackintosh and rescue his reputation from being just the darling stylist of the new Glasgow.

Ask anyone today in Glasgow's Sauchiehall Street who Charles Rennie Mackintosh was and the chances are that they will proudly describe the work of a stylish furniture designer, an interior decorator, an artist or even a jeweller. But few will sing the praises of Mackintosh the architect.

Locally, the great Glasgow builder is now best known as the designer of 1990s souvenir kitsch. To celebrate Glasgow's accolade as 1990 City of Culture, the advertisers Saatchi and Saatchi devised its slogan, 'A lot of Glasgowing on', in pastiche Mackintosh lettering. Their metropolitan provincialism continually failed to grasp the essence of Mackintosh's squared-up graphics over a year of embarrassingly inept billboards and brochures. It helped fuel the demand for puce and four-square 'Repro Mac', turning the boutiques of Sauchiehall Street into hoards of what can only be called 'Saatchihall Mockintosh'. Admittedly, the Sauchiehall Street Centre of the 1980s had already set the tune in its collision of unabashed 'Mockintosh' with Belgian Art Nouveau. Here little tiles in chequered squares nudged wilting roses; here a Mackintosh rafter, there a Mackintosh lamp; details derived from different Mackintosh buildings jostle together into an ersatz scotch broth, provoking visual indigestion.

Could this be the same Scottish swing of the kitsch that took the poems of Burns and the works of Scott and mulched them down into a midden of tea-towel schmaltz? It is hard to see the same souvenir buyers appreciating the architectural significance of the Glasgow School of Art across the street above them. Will they see Mackintosh's masterwork as just another grubby old building? Where in all this is the creator of such magical architectural spaces as the library of the Glasgow School of Art? Who still appreciates Mackintosh's mastery in manipulating light; his skill in creating such telling shifts in scale, his ability to counterpoint large expanses of undecorated surface with small strategically placed exquisite detail? What has become of Mackintosh the architect? Well, at least his buildings survived the 1960s.

It is hard to imagine now that in the Glasgow of the 1960s Mackintosh was a nearly forgotten figure. Even local architects then had little good to say about his buildings or his efforts at simplifying once ornate Victorian spaces. Journalists made jokes about his spiny tea room chairs, forgetting that straight backs then were an essential part of an upright life. Mackintosh to them was just another long-haired arty crafty who had hit the bottle before drifting into obscurity as a water-colourist abroad.

In the late 1960s the trajectory of Glasgow's inner ring road seemed to have been planned to destroy as many Mackintosh buildings as possible. Although the School of Art on Garnethill was well above the bulldozers, it was not immune from lamentable planning decisions. A vertical slab of corduroy concrete rose to thwart the horizontal School of Art across Renfrew Street. Following the success of the 1968 Mackintosh centenary exhibition, which toured abroad after its successful run at the Edinburgh Festival, I remember asking:

> But what of Glasgow, the city he made famous? The place with the permanent outdoor exhibition of his buildings. Well, there was a rumour that Glasgow might mark the centenary by knocking down a Mackintosh building or two. They didn't quite do that. Though the decline of all Mackintosh's buildings in the city continued. No help was given to clean and restore the fabric of the Glasgow School of Art. And those tram-pole lights and cables still criss-crossed one of the most famous façades in modern architecture. Visitors to Glasgow even found it hard to photograph. Some dodged into a building site across Renfrew Street to avoid the poles. But now the site is sealed. An intimidating block has arisen to dwarf the school. In its towering arrogance it symbolizes the regard in which Mackintosh is held in Glasgow by the governors of the School of Art who commissioned it, by Glasgow Corporation who permitted it and by Mackintosh's old firm, Honeyman and Keppie, who designed it. But the cruellest irony of all, they are going to call it Newbery Tower. It was Fra Newbery who gave Mackintosh his first (and last) major commission – the Glasgow School of Art. When future students try and paint in Mackintosh's studios they will have a dose of reflected irony; south light rebounding off the 'Newbery Tower' will defeat the very functionalism of his original north-light-seeking windows.

'Mackintosh / The Present Situation in Glasgow'
Scottish International, No. 8, February 1970

The Sauchiehall Street Centre.
Photograph: Murray Grigor

In the early 1960s I worked in Glasgow as a film editor with the BBC, whose Scottish headquarters had already all but obliterated any trace of Mackintosh's hand in the creation of his firm's Queen Margaret's Medical College. Little more than the staircase tower now remains with its massive iron gates, which curiously seem more reminiscent of early Gaudi than Mackintosh.

In those days I shared a flat with a journalist, Bill Williams. As students we had made a film together on crusader castles, which got me into the BBC and Bill a job as leader writer on the *Glasgow Herald*. The old *Herald* office was one of the first buildings that Mackintosh worked on and his furniture there was often blamed for bruising writers' shins, or so Alistair Phillips wrote disparagingly in his column from time to time. One of his worst put-downs ridiculed our newly formed 'Friends of Toshie', a preservation pressure group which Bill and I had formed after a trip to Barcelona.

For months I had been pestering the head of programmes at the BBC with my script on Mackintosh, but he was reluctant to consider a film on architecture, never mind an unknown Glasgow architect. He had found a recent Ken Russell piece on Antonio Gaudi interesting, so I proposed a film contrasting the great Mediterranean exponent of Art Nouveau or *Modernismo* with his northern counterpart. Why not introduce a little of Mackintosh's architecture and contrast it with Gaudi's more ectoplasmic work in a programme that compared the two mercantile cities of Glasgow and Barcelona? As a compromise, I was allowed to shoot a little film comparing the cities of Glasgow and Barcelona, into which we could slip a sequence on the architecture of Mackintosh and Gaudi.

Interior: The Sauchiehall Street Centre.

The *Amigos de Gandí* in Barcelona were enthusiastic and helpful. They had pioneered a popular reassessment of this great Catalan architect and had helped initiate the building programme on his soaring unfinished masterwork, the *Sagrada Familia* cathedral. Unlike Mackintosh, Gaudi had always had his champions. In the 1920s his dreamlike waves of broken crockery and molten ironmongery had inspired the Surrealists. They had heard of Gaudi's 'comestible architecture' through the writings of his precocious fellow Catalan, Salvador Dali. What, we wondered, would Dali have thought of Mackintosh, whose taut forms must surely be the polar opposite of Gaudi's ectoplasmic coils.

There were two pumas asleep in the corner of the dazzling white studio where we waited. Then in came Dali with Robert Schmutzler's fat book on Art Nouveau. A coloured plate of the leaded glass doors of Mackintosh's Willow Tea Room lay open in his hands. When he heard that they were now part of a Glasgow store called Daly's, Dali was ecstatic. The book dropped to the floor with a resounding blast. The pumas leapt. 'A sound sublime,' Dali sighed, as he threw his arms apart in a silent-movie gesture. 'Daly! Dali! The doors are mine. For me you buy them for famous Dali museum.'

The threat of exporting the doors did much to awaken interest in the state of the Willow Tea Room back home. For not even Dali's bizarre imagination could have dreamt up the surrealist use to which Miss Cranston's Room de Luxe had fallen. Against Margaret Macdonald's gesso panel of two sad spinsters, inspired by Rossetti's sonnet on widowhood, future brides were being fitted out in wedding gowns. The weeping Willow's inner sanctum had become the Bridal Suite of Daly's department store.

Although our twin-city programme had petered out, I had now revised my film script to concentrate on Mackintosh. By this time, I had grown friendly with the most remarkable man in recent Mackintosh history. Andrew McLaren Young was Richmond Professor of Fine Art at Glasgow University, and keeper of the contents of the Mackintoshes' last home in Southpark Avenue, which the University had recently demolished to make way for a new refectory. Andrew was planning his major Mackintosh centenary exhibition for the 1968 Edinburgh Festival and his work on this would soon progress alongside my film, the one helping the other.

This was before the days of responding to market forces, when the Scottish Arts Council showed active cultural leadership. They saw this film as an essential part of the Mackintosh celebrations. It was just the creative spur I needed to leave BBC Scotland. BBC indifference, I soon found out, was a local problem and was not reflected in the south. Stephen Hearst, the head of BBC arts programmes in London, had heard about my film and arranged a meeting with Hew Weldon, the editor of their flagship arts programme 'Monitor'. As a refugee from Vienna, Hearst knew all about Mackintosh through his interest in Josef Hoffmann and the Vienna Secession. But Hew was baffled. 'Charles Rennie who?' Once again Gaudi came to the rescue. In Ken Russell's film, which Weldon narrated, I remembered a reference to Mackintosh. 'Quite right, clever chap.' We got the post-production costs for a network BBC2 transmission.

Among the few Mackintosh enthusiasts who attached themselves to Andrew McLaren Young's department was a postgraduate from Naples, Bruno del Priore, who seemed to spend all his time making precise measured drawings of Mackintosh furniture. He sent these back in batches to Filippo Alison, the head of design in Naples University, who was having them made up as replicas as part of his research into Mackintosh design. Students occupying the university buildings considered the cause worthy enough to allow a consignment of drawings past the picket lines during the 1968 sit-in.

When I stopped over in Italy to visit Filippo, he immediately swept me out through the evening traffic along the Bay of Naples to Torre Annunziata. We soon arrived at a courtyard, passed barrels of wine, climbed worn stone steps, and there we were on the threshold of the workshop belonging to the cabinet-maker Domenico Guida. Like a safety curtain rising on a breath-taking stage set, the door creaked open to reveal an attic room full of black and white Mackintosh chairs. Remember: this was a time when it was almost impossible to see Mackintosh's furniture outside the Glasgow School of Art. To see a whole array of them in a loft, under the bright light and sharp shadows of southern Italy, was like a de Chirico dream painting. There was the curved lattice screen of the cashier's chair from the Willow Tea Room, caught in a shaft of sunlight, scattering its grid of small squares across the sawdust floor. As we tiptoed around, bone-white chairs became back-lit silhouettes. Dark-stained high-backs (with Mackintosh's witty hand-slot set impossibly high for lifting) emerged from the shadows to be caught in the last rays of the sinking sun. Filippo's English was as minimal as my Italian. But as glasses of *Mondragone*, the cabinet-maker's own Vesuvian wine, worked their magic, words seemed unimportant. Filippo reached for a high-back chair and played it like a double bass. Here was no dry academic; more a maestro. Four chairs in a half circle seemed poised to play a string quartet.

It was Filippo who relaunched Mackintosh as a designer, turning the output of an architect, who had died in the 1920s, into an almost contemporary designer of the 1970s. He persuaded the furniture manufacturer Cesare Cassina to help fund an exhibition of Guida's Mackintosh replicas. This exhibition became one of the great successes of the 1973 Milan Triennale, along with another in the Cassina showroom, where high-backed Ingram Street tea room chairs flanked a giant photo mural of Mackintosh. The response from designers, public and press was so overwhelming that

Cesare Cassina immediately struck up a deal with Andrew McLaren Young on behalf of the University of Glasgow to reproduce the chairs.

As a result, Mackintosh furniture became part of the Cassina *I Maestri* collection, which already included twentieth-century classics by Marcel Breuer, Le Corbusier and Mies van der Rohe. Cassina has now taken Mackintosh across the world. Over four thousand replicas have been made of the Willow lattice-back alone, with the School of Art initially receiving royalties and subsequently travelling scholarships and an annual prize. The University's royalties, appropriately, have made a substantial contribution to the care and storage of its Mackintosh archive.

In 1970 the only Mackintosh exhibit at the Kelvingrove Gallery was a single ladder-back chair and that was used only as an anachronistic prop in an Edwardian costume display. The few other chairs in the museum's collection suffered, out of the public view, by being sat on daily in the staff canteen. Bruno and I tried to interest the director in showing the whole Mackintosh Cassina range as an exhibition imaginatively devised by Filippo. We were told rather brusquely that this museum never showed reproductions, only originals. A strange excuse, Bruno and I thought, as we made our way out of the gallery, past ranks of dinosaurs. Were they originals? Instead, this show became the highlight of the year at the Museum of Modern Art, New York. Mackintosh became the darling of the international press, over forty years after his death.

Photograph: Murray Grigor

As Mackintosh's designs re-entered the world of international design, most of the architect's buildings were under threat of demolition back in Glasgow. Even his Scotland Street School, with its castle-like towers of leaded glass window bays, was under threat. And the interiors of the Ingram Street tea room continued to erode in a damp storeroom.

In the centre of the city, a shopfront said it all: 'The Mackintosh Discount House' in Ingram Street. Once one of Miss Cranston's most appealing and spatially inventive tea rooms, it stared back into George Square in its final death throes. In a previous incarnation it had been known as 'The Rennie Mackintosh Gift Shoppe'. In those days the assistants were called Miss Rennie and Miss Mackintosh and the carpet was Mackintosh all right, but of the tartan variety; which was not quite what the architect had in mind. What was left of the curving woodwork and decorated panels cowered behind swags of tourist kitsch. Mackintosh's internationally famous China Tea Room was now a clutter of cardboard boxes. Mr Zederbaum, the shopkeeper, was hardly to blame. He had rented the disbanded tea rooms from the city, who had bought the Mackintosh-designed rooms for *cultural purposes* years before. This seemingly enlightened civic act was instigated by the persistence of Thomas Howarth, whose influential book hailed Mackintosh as a pioneer of the Modern Movement. When Howarth left for Canada, Glasgow soon reneged on its promise.

Before the shoppekeeper's lease expired I remember suggesting to William Wells, the curator of the then still buried Burrell Collection, that the Ingram Street tea rooms could be rehoused as his museum restaurant, whenever the long proposed gallery was built. Sir William Burrell was a shipowner who built up his art collection on the scale of the great American collectors. In fact, when Hearst was forced to sell parts of his plunder, it was Burrell who brought many of his architectural fragments back to Europe in their still unpacked crates. In the new Burrell Collection building it would be all right to patch in Hearst's medieval portals, but not apparently to incorporate doors and screens by Glasgow's Mackintosh. 'This wouldn't be appropriate,' Wells said, 'since there was a special thrill to experiencing Mackintosh's spaces of light and magic by entering them from sooty dark Glasgow streets.' There was something in this, I thought, provided the streets remained. 'Furthermore,' Wells added, 'the Burrell Collection was a finite one to which nothing could be added.' How strange, then, that ten years later the Burrell Trustees bought the Warwick vase, a much-restored eighteenth-century wonder of Roman sculpture. Despite the fact that classical art was an area that Burrell had almost ignored in building up his vast collection, it was selected as the symbol for the Burrell on all its brochures.

Sadly, the guardians of the city's culture refused an offer for the Ingram Street tea rooms interiors from the Smithsonian Institute's Cooper-Hewitt Museum of Design in New York. There they could have been installed for the delight of millions. It would have been a curiously appropriate reincarnation, for the museum was once the Fifth Avenue mansion of Scots-born Andrew Carnegie.

When the Ingram Street lease finally lapsed, the fittings were removed, catalogued and lodged in a store at the instigation of the Planning Department. Happily, over the last few years, a number of pieces have been put back together and occasionally exhibited. But will the mysterious interrelationships of Mackintosh's complementary spaces ever be restored? Will those strange progressions from light to shade ever be experienced again? Will we ever be able to move again under the soaring balcony of the Oak Room, with its echoes of the Glasgow School of Art library, and enter the Cloister Room, with its stylized Chinese Gothic tracery and its witty arches of wavy patterns in strident colours?

Before all this was lost, the city treasurer Samuels gave me an interview in what was left of the Ingram interiors. As we stood next to the cashier's confessional booth-like desk, he told me that Mackintosh was grossly overrated. There were carved chairs in Glasgow Cathedral of far greater value. None the less, on behalf of the city, he did promise that the decorative parts of these interiors would be removed and re-erected in Mackintosh's Scotland Street School. When Andrew McLaren Young heard this, he felt that official attitudes were warming just a little. A few years earlier, he had been shown around a store under the City Chambers. High-back Ingram Street chairs seemed to have been pitched and bashed together into broken parts, as though they were the victims of some strange indoor Highland Games. Much of the furniture was in poor repair. When Andrew asked why they were kept in such a state, 'What's needed in here is a fire', the custodian menaced him, with a snarling 'r'. Even then, before Mackintosh furniture broke saleroom records, Andrew estimated these chairs were worth thousands to the citizens of Glasgow.

In 1973, on the initiative of the New Glasgow Society, the Charles Rennie Mackintosh Society was formed and the tide of disregard was finally turned. The society was active in helping to deflect the new ring road from demolishing Mackintosh's Martyrs Public School. The planned elevated concrete viaduct was diverted away from Queen's Cross Church (CRM 1897–99). In 1977 the Society undertook the care and restoration of this important building which with the help of Glasgow District Council and many others saved it from dereliction. Almost all of its original features are preserved and it is currently used as the Society's international headquarters with a small exhibition area, reference library and shop for the enthusiast. Directed by the indefatigable Patricia Douglas, the Society now has a membership of over 1500 world-wide and plays a leading role in the dissemination of knowledge and information on Mackintosh and his work.

Symbolically, it was the reconstruction of the architect's own home as part of the University of Glasgow's Hunterian Art Gallery that finally reversed Mackintosh's reputation in Glasgow. Parallel to this, the city itself was beginning to undergo its own risorgimento through a more inspired rebuilding programme, bringing people back to live in its centre and re-creating life after dark.

Private patronage had enabled Andrew McLaren Young to go ahead on the rebuilding of Mackintosh's home. William Whitfield, architect of the soaring towers of the new library block and Hunterian Art Gallery, grafted on to it the shell of Mackintosh's original terrace house, including the windows he had broken out 'for my wife, Mistress Margaret, so that she can watch the sunsets'.

Sadly, Andrew McLaren Young died before the building was completed. Fitments meticulously restored by Hector Grant and Brian MacKerracher are now seamlessly in place in those extraordinary white rooms. The whole is a great memorial to Andrew's largely forgotten energetic endeavour and the campaign he kept alive throughout the 1960s.

School of Art and the 'Newbery Tower', right. Photograph: Glasgow School of Art

As if the shadowing Newbery Tower were not insulting enough, the governors of the Glasgow School of Art wrought another monster on Mackintosh's masterpiece. This time the slab was on its side: a hideous concrete bridge of sighs to straddle Renfrew Street. This crassly insensitive affront to Mackintosh's most famous elevation now menaces the soaringly uplifting library windows of the west front in its commercial-building-like ugly squatness.

For a building that is now rising to a century of continuous use, the Glasgow School of Art has worn triumphantly well. Credit should go to the Governors and Directors through such changing times for keeping Mackintosh's not entirely practical building intact as a working school. Although nothing but creative demolition can be done in the short term to treat the plague of monsters that now surround it, it was reassuring when the ugly lamp standards, with their swags of wiring, and most of the street-level junkitecture were swept away on the approach to Glasgow's *annus mirabilis* of 1990. But not for long. They have now been replaced by replica Mackintosh ones, derived from the *c* 1915 drawings in the Patrick Geddes Collection of Strathclyde University. These are a wholly inappropriate and confusing addition; a really odd idea to extend the *oeuvre* of Mackintosh. In fact there is no need for lamp poles. Street lighting could easily be achieved from the building itself, leaving Mackintosh's standards and curved railings as telling silhouettes.

My film, *Mackintosh*, was first shown at the Edinburgh Festival in 1968 and accompanied the exhibition wherever it went and was lucky enough to win a clutch of prizes. It was selected for the Venice Biennale and as a result I met many young architects and designers who all admired Mackintosh as an architects' architect. They included the American Richard Meier, the Japanese Arata Isozaki and the Austrian Hans Hollein, who invited me to devise a series of short films for the Bicentennial opening of the Cooper-Hewitt Museum, New York.

In 1970 I persuaded the BBC to let me make a follow-up programme to question why Glasgow had done so little for Mackintosh, following the critical acclaim of his work in Edinburgh, London, Darmstadt, Vienna, Venice, Milan and New York. After all, Glasgow was Mackintosh's home town and the only one to have a permanent exhibition of the architect's works. But could Mackintosh's buildings even be considered permanent in a city which seemed bent on committing urbicide in daily spasms of civic self-hatred? District after district tore itself apart, street by street, without any regard for their architectural merit. Tenements by Alexander Thomson were bludgeoned down, including his masterful Blackie's building in Stanhope Street, with its Talwin Morris studio interior. I saved some of the Morris apple-green cabinets with their characteristic tear-drop brasswork, and for a few years these languished in a Glasgow University corridor. A cut-down version still survives there under a surprisingly inappropriate coat of Mackintosh-like white paint. Under Blackie's vandalized rafters I found the building's original working drawings and handed them on to the Fine Art Department. It would not be long, I thought, before it would be Mackintosh's turn.

Nowadays it is hard to imagine a time in Glasgow when Mackintosh was treated with total disregard. How then did the international reputation and the strength of a Glasgow builder get so confused in the city of his birth as a designer of tea towels and coffee mugs? It is an insignificant complaint when we are confronted with the 'Mockintosh' of the new built environment. All over town streets have sprung up with roses nudged by squares in fours. Even staid Edinburgh, a city whose *good taste* never tolerated decadent Art Nouveau in the past, is now enjoying its own Mockintosh fling. Perhaps as a challenge to the Big Mac at the other end of Princes Street, a Wimpy hamburger outlet had done itself up like some transfigured Cranston tea room, with high-back chairs in marbled plastic.

Today the underexposed architect has become the overexposed designer. In grasping the rose, Scotland seems to have forgotten Mackintosh's genius as a magical manipulator of light and space, the stuff of architecture. Even discounting the pastiche Mockintosh, what could be done to reveal Mackintosh's achievement in the round? Through the Charles Rennie Mackintosh Society my idea was to invite six major architects back to Glasgow to help square his reputation in the city of his birth. We asked each of them to design a tribute as an attempt to fix Mackintosh as the seminal *architect* he really is among many of the leading architects working today. My colleague, the architect Richard Murphy, gathered fifth-year students from the Mackintosh School of Architecture and supervised the tricky business of constructing the architects' installations.

Our aim was to invite architects who were attracted to different aspects of Mackintosh's work. In the end we were rewarded with a wonderfully disparate group in Edward Cullinan (England), Aldo van Eyck (The Netherlands), Hans Hollein (Austria), Arata Isozaki (Japan), Leon Krier (Luxembourg/England) and Stanley Tigerman (USA). Each architect devised an ingenious exhibit on contrasting aspects of Mackintosh's work, designed to be placed either outside or inside the School of Art. The installations were as divergent as the architects' views on Mackintosh's architectural significance.

Ted Cullinan chose to remodel the director's bathroom which included the design of a free-standing functioning shower. Aldo van Eyck challenged the need for the school's fire doors installed in the 1960s as well as celebrating the mirrored window fillets in the bay of the Willow Tea Room. In the library, Hans Hollein hung a set of evolving grids, a series of gilded transformations which he saw as emblematic of the gothic, the floral and modernist tendencies in Mackintosh's architecture. Under the Japanese-like roof beams of the upper west studio, Arata Isozaki surrounded a ceramic-topped table with four chairs, their Mackintosh-like high backs metamorphosed into the curves of Marilyn Monroe. Leon Krier devised a finial to 'complete' what he considered to be the 'unfinished' tower above the director's room. Stanley Tigerman attached a series of grids to counterpoint Mackintosh's use of balanced asymmetry.

As much in memory of Mackintosh's journey through Italy when a student, as a homage across time from a designer to a master, Filippo Alison devised a double-action Neapolitan coffee percolator and showed a giant replica of it in the entrance hall.

To add to all this, James Stirling exhibited drawings of his own work and spoke of the impact the school had on him as an off-duty soldier garrisoned in Maryhill Barracks during the Second World War. Stirling pondered at the exhibition opening that Mackintosh's school, in all its complexities, might even have seeded in him the idea of a career in architecture.

Another display included the suite of six woodcuts dedicated to Charles Rennie Mackintosh by Eduardo Paolozzi in 1976. These haunting images transpose the curved lines, chequers and the sudden switches of darkness and lightness of Mackintosh's architecture so seamlessly into another art form. We were thrilled that Sir Eduardo accepted our invitation to open the exhibition that summer's night in June. As the large turnout spread themselves across Renfrew Street, the dilemma of Mackintosh and Glasgow faced us from the steps of the Art School. Somehow Mackintosh's reputation could cross the world, but not this street. The assemblage of truly appalling buildings that faced us said it all.

As the Austrian architect Hans Hollein reveals in his interview, none of the great early-twentieth-century architects was discussed in the architecture schools in the 1950s and 1960s. As a student, Hollein had learnt about the work of Hoffmann and Mackintosh from his own researches. He came to

Glasgow to see and experience the buildings at first hand. Arata Isozaki relates a similar story from Japan. None of these young architects could understand why Glasgow was so indifferent to Mackintosh's work at the time.

Accompanying the international architects' installations was a symposium to discuss Mackintosh's relevance to architecture today in terms of internationalism and regionalism, innovation and tradition. The symposium was part of a major three-day conference organized by the Charles Rennie Mackintosh Society in association with the Glasgow School of Art. Heated discussion, tantalizingly squeezed into a single morning, left a lot of questions hanging in the air. To develop the arguments more fully, we decided to talk to the participating architects in turn and the result is this collection of interviews.

If the 1990 conference and exhibitions did no more than disentangle the false Mockintosh from the real Mackintosh and reappraise the achievement of the architect who, sixty years after his death, has become a contemporary force in world architecture, then it will have been worthwhile.

Linlithgow Palace, *c.*1504. The smooth masonry of the west range presages Mackintosh's Glasgow School of Art.
Photograph: Murray Grigor

EDWARD CULLINAN

I FIRST SAW a picture of the Glasgow School of Art during a history slide lecture when I was at the School of Architecture in Cambridge in the early 1950s. It was that usual dismal picture of the north elevation which David Roberts showed as part of his lecture on the Arts and Crafts movement. So that fairly buried Mackintosh as far as I was concerned, as a sort of aberration in the far north. At that time Cambridge University was a relic of the Arts and Crafts movement. Gropius had applied to be chairman of the school before the war, but was turned down in favour of Lutyens's assistant and went over to the other Cambridge in the States.

Gamble House, Pasadena, California, 1908. Greene & Greene.
Photograph: Marvin Rand

My perception of Mackintosh changed when I saw the work of Greene & Greene and Maybeck in California. Mackintosh fits absolutely into that tradition. Taken together with my interest in Mendelsohn, any tendency I had to be a reductionist, modernist or purist began to be moved very strongly in the direction of expressionism. Berkeley 1956/7 were my most formative years. That was the time when Esther McCoy put on her first Five California Architects exhibition.

Then I came back to England and worked with Lasdun, who is a romantic if he did but know it. We argued quite a lot but did some good work together. He gave me the job to do at Minster Lovell, which started me looking at the responsive gentle romantic stream in the history of modernism. This is a very powerful stream which sends you back to look at Mackintosh. Mackintosh and Wright seem to represent the mannerist period of the Arts and Crafts movement with late Lutyens its baroque. But Mackintosh adds a fantastic sense of style and grace and brings in powerful European influences. If you take a Philip Webb chair or a William Morris chair it looks straight back into history. Mackintosh took pieces of wood and put them together in a way

OPPOSITE
'Readymix Concrete Headquarters, Berkshire, by Edward Cullinan Architects, 1991 – the celebrating of necessity.'
Photograph: Martin Charles

which I think leads to De Stijl, which is actually about taking bits apart.

What were your impressions when you first visited the Glasgow School of Art?

Well, my first impression was of being taken out of Andy MacMillan's* office across the street directly into the diagonal lecture theatre under the library. So I went in the wrong way, but what a beautiful way round, through that door which holds the steep incline of the street under that wonderful bay-windowed façade.

The next day I walked through it, up that stairway which is also an art gallery. It's a fantastically good plan for a drop site, with its studios on a hilltop set beautifully off the gallery. Then at one end there are those more private rooms and at the other end there's his library soaring through the section. It's wonderful because the gallery and studios in section are reduced on the next storey to just studios with a cat-walk or 'hen run' along the top.

You have sometimes been described as an architect of the section. Is that what attracts you about the School of Art?

Well yes, I describe in sections because that's the easiest way to draw the space you feel. I have also been described as an Arts and Crafts architect because I talk a lot about the arts and crafts. But I am not. No, I like the romantic stream in modern architecture because I come from Mackintosh, Wright, Greene & Greene to Rietveld's Schroeder House and Le Corbusier's Maisons Jaoul and Ronchamp. Expressionist, expressive, romantic modernism is undergoing a fantastic revival just now in the schools of architecture, much to my delight, like the new stuff by Peter Salter. It's an extremely powerful and valuable way to think because you are saying architecture is the celebration of necessity and the celebration of opportunity and Mackintosh is that absolutely.

How do you answer the criticisms of the school's narrow entrance and asymmetry?

Leon Krier confused the word door with the word entrance when he criticized its narrowness. You have to understand that the whole central piece of this building, with its wide curving walled steps, is its entrance.

The whole building is a very subtle balanced asymmetry, an asymmetric

* Professor Andrew MacMillan, Head of the Mackintosh School of Architecture, Glasgow.

entrance in an asymmetric façade of four and three studio windows on each level. The elevations are different from one another, reflecting the streets they face and their functions within, each informing the other. The rear elevation is rendered, as many of the backs of Glasgow buildings are. Into the top and sides of this rendered craggy castle on the hill Mackintosh engaged subtle stone pieces from the masonry elevations. Thus one elevation informs the other and creates a wonderfully balanced asymmetry.

If there was a competition for the School of Art today, would they be able to find and afford the craftsmen?

We are not bereft of craftsmen today. We don't pay them enough but when we do they make the most fantastic work, brilliant craftsmanship. We have had beautiful brickwork in our RMC [Ready Mix Concrete Ltd] headquarters building and superb joinery, wonderfully done.

Given the chance Mackintosh, like Wright, would design everything, yet you also describe him as a pragmatist. How do you reconcile these two ideas?

Mackintosh is much more pragmatic than Wright. Wright invented the most profound moment in domestic architecture in his plan for the Ward Willits' house and Mackintosh never did anything like that. I am told that the Scotland

Minster Lovell Conference Centre, Wiltshire, 1973.
Edward Cullinan Architects.
Photograph: Courtesy of Edward Cullinan

Street School plan was handed to Mackintosh. The Hill House has an absolutely standard Arts and Crafts gallery plan, which could have been done by anyone from Philip Webb onwards.

Although Mackintosh's plans weren't inventive he designed the places. When compared with Wright he was an absolutely sublime designer of details. Look at Wright's furniture and his dumb compass drawn leaded glass and all that.

Do you think that Mackintosh is fundamentally Scottish?

No, I don't. Mackintosh may be perceived as such because it's easier to have a romantic idea of a Scot or an Irishman than an Englishman. If you come from north of Hadrian's Wall and have a staggering history forced on you by colonization you have the amazing romantic dream of Celts; of general Highland mayhem behind you. It makes it much easier to be nationalistic than it is for English people. I know this because I am half Irish and have a much more romantic idea of myself as an Irishman, than as an Englishman.

Can you talk a little about your installation?

Off the director's room, which is a wonderful asymmetric composition, there's a washroom which has been well and thoroughly butchered since Mackintosh left it.

In this very sad and forlorn space my team, Roddy Langmuir, Johnnie Cadell and I, found that Mackintosh's wash-stand had been hurled into the corner and everything generally had been mucked about, with a repulsive plastic shower and an extremely nasty streamlined loo that seemed to have been designed to move fast through space. Sanitary catalogue misery. It's what happens when you forget to love things and buy for convenience only.

So we wondered what would happen if we gave ourselves a new brief. Like a lot of architects, we started with indulgent and extravagant ideas. We found that there was space beneath the stairs. So we devised a shower door that could rise up into this space with pulleys and weights. Andy MacMillan, was deeply shocked. He wanted no tampering with Mackintosh fabric. We tried sinking it into the floor, and other pathetic meanderings that architects are prone to have. Then it dawned on us that when Mackintosh designed kitchens and bathrooms he designed them as though they were dining rooms and living rooms with furniture standing in space. So we decided that the

LEFT
'That door which holds the steep incline of the street.'
West entrance.
Photograph: T & R Annan & Sons

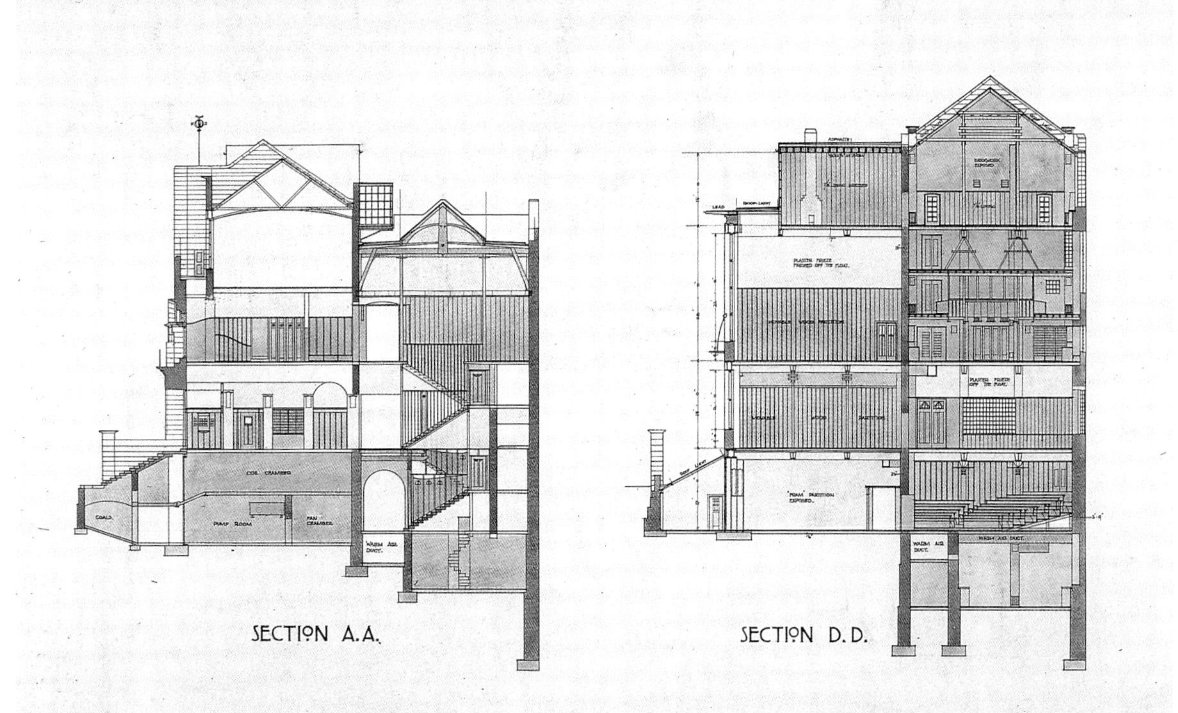

BELOW
Two drawings showing sections through the School of Art.
Left: section AA shows the entrance, stair, gallery and director's office study. Note the hen run 'bypass' above the gallery roof and the SW top studio.
Right: section DD shows the lecture theatre and library.
Photograph: Glasgow School of Art

Top left: N and W facades.
Photograph: Glasgow School of Art

Top right: W and S facades.
Photograph: T & R Annan & Sons.

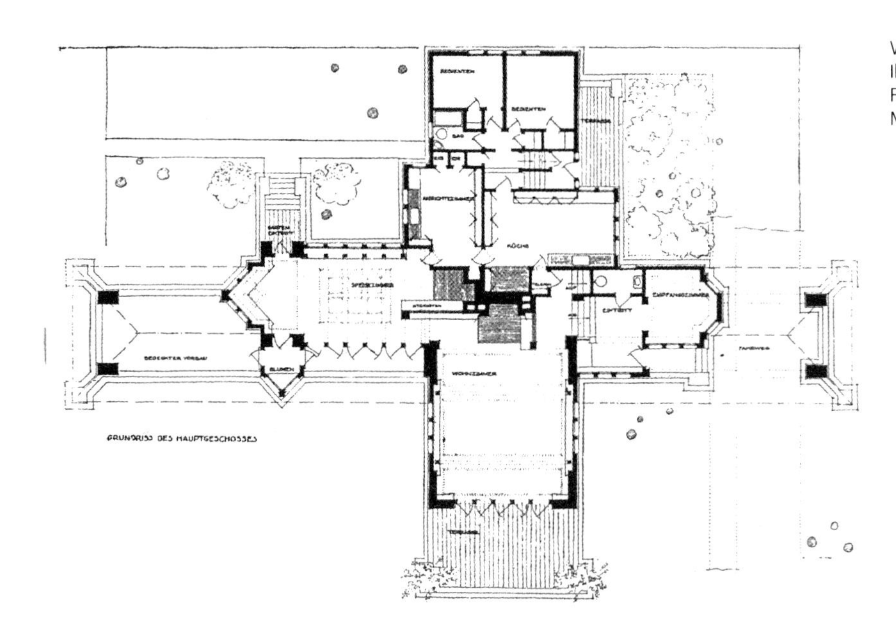

Ward Willits' House, Highland Park, Illinois 1901.
Frank Lloyd Wright.
Main floor plan.

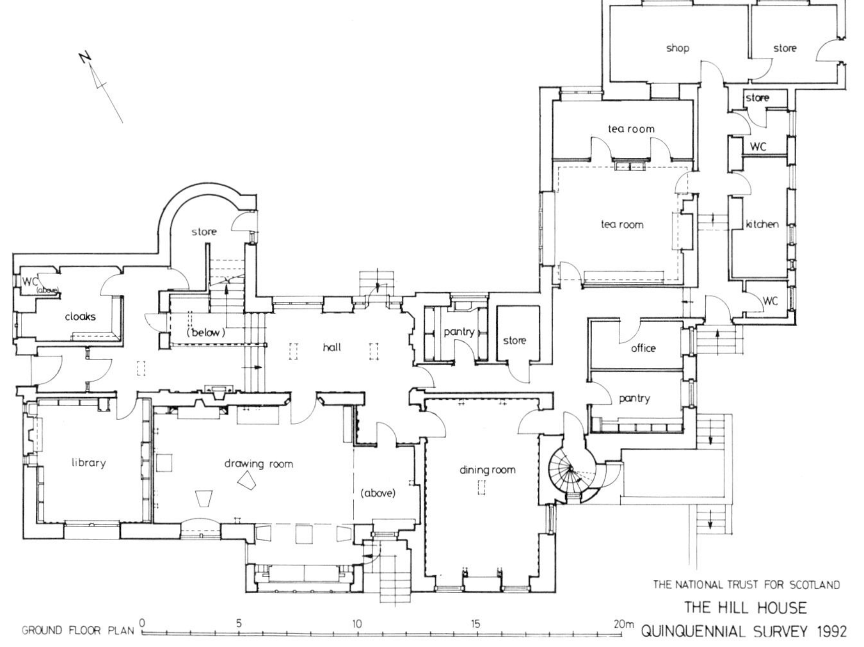

The Hill House, Helensburgh, 1902–3.
C R Mackintosh.
Ground floor plan.

OPPOSITE
Bottom left: E and N facades.
Bottom right: S and E facades.
Photograph: Hunterian Art Gallery, University of Glasgow, Mackintosh Collection

OPPOSITE
Shower at bathroom,
The Hill House.
Photograph: National Trust for Scotland.

Cullinan shower at the Glasgow School of Art.
Photograph: Up-front

Detail of handle.
Photograph: Up-front

shower should go centrally where the basin had been. We then made a new version of the Mackintosh basin, which had long since disappeared.

The shower we devised is a simple object with four columns rising to a cornice, with exactly the same profile as the cornice in the director's office next door. Mackintosh had a great love of a tight curve followed by a long lazy one, which we followed.

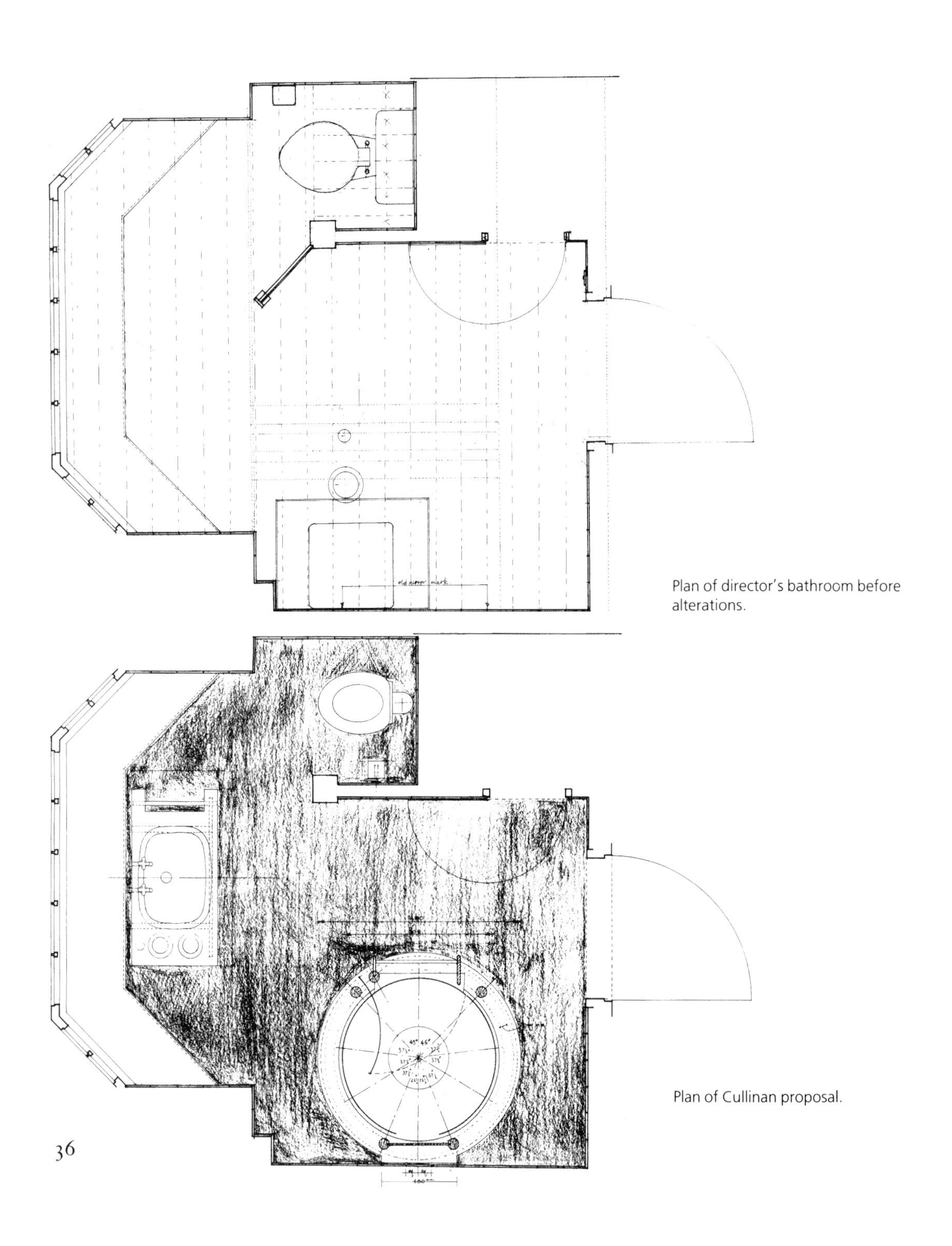

Plan of director's bathroom before alterations.

Plan of Cullinan proposal.

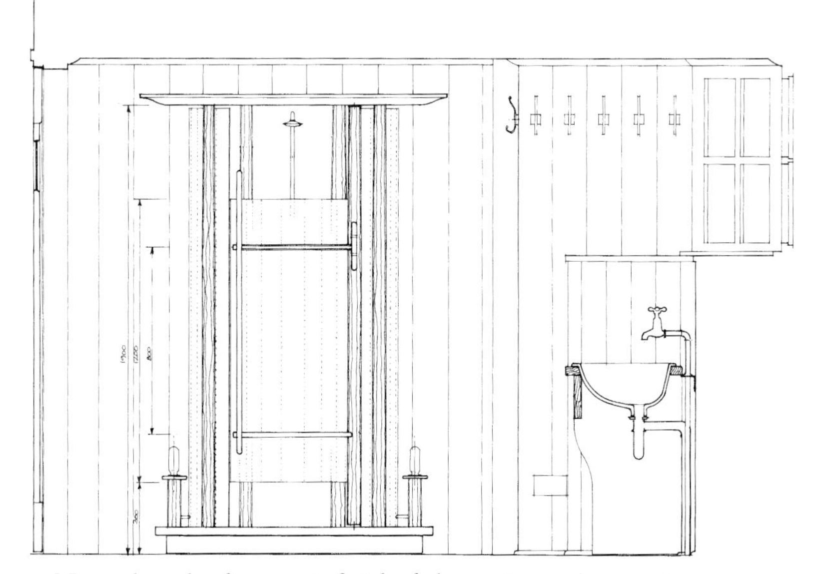

Section/elevation of new shower and repositioned wash-hand basin.

Now when the director is finished showering and wet, a dry towel comes in on a handle. We placed three coloured marbles in the door handle, green, blue and red, which I chose sitting on the floor in Hamleys, 10p, 5p and the smallest, three for 2p. That was our way of making those lovely little coloured details that Mackintosh put into his buildings.

Our lesson from Mackintosh was to try to create elegant objects as free-standing furniture in space.

Why do you think Mackintosh's career was so short?

My theory is that Mackintosh needed Honeyman & Keppie to organize his work. I know how pricelessly valuable good management is to an architect from my own practice of around thirty people. We have architects who, while taking part in designs, also cause them to happen. I think Mackintosh lost that back-up. There must be an amazing amount of research to be done on Mackintosh's relationship with his partners. I think it's absolutely nuts to try and decide whether Mackintosh hit the bottle or not. It's much more important to know what he was getting from Honeyman & Keppie. I bet there were cases of Mackintosh asking builders to do things differently and the builders would come back to someone in the office and say, 'You know it's going to cost a lot more if we do what Mr Mackintosh asks for?' There must have been a lot of back-up in the office. I know things like this must have happened because that's my imagined explanation of why Mackintosh stops functioning well after he leaves Glasgow.

167

LEON KRIER

I AM NOT a fan of Mackintosh but the exterior of the school is an arresting masterpiece. As with Horta and Hoffmann, it is impossible not to be impressed by the quality of their work, but as exotic dishes, I get quickly tired with the languid obsessiveness which pervades their products, be they a spoon or a city block.

One of the things which irritates me no end (an irritation which is probably intended, but that doesn't justify it) is the miserly meanness of the main entrance. The stumpiness of the polygonal tower and the plain silliness of the bird crowning it all; of course it is all this which creates the maximum tension with the grand order of the windows, but it is also like entering a cathedral through a cottage door. To me this entrance is like a face crowning a good body, but shrivelled by some inexplicable anxiety. It is exhorting the young people entering this temple of learning and apprenticeship: 'We up here are a cosy little arts and crafts club, we are quite full of ourselves and we are so much better than everybody else but beware, we keep all this to ourselves; it may look like it but, hell, this is not a public building – and please keep out.' Anyway, this building talks a lot: a different story to different people. I personally feel that something is missing on the tower and I would be delighted if my idea could be built, even if it will be around only for a few weeks.

A return to sound building techniques.' Office and apartment building, Rue de Vauginard, Paris, 1975.
Christan Langlais.
Photographs: Courtesy of Leon Krier

I think Mackintosh was a very talented person and I get pleasure out of his buildings. There is no doubt that he had good traditional roots. But he had too many trivial obsessions to be taken seriously as an influence on architecture today. The strange extravagance of his work, which has been applauded to heaven for being anti-hierarchical, was really something of an aberration. His real value was that he was a traditional architect who added

OPPOSITE
'The scale of a factory with the door of a cottage.'
Photograph: Glasgow School of Art

some odd details to his buildings. There is nothing revolutionary about his work and his private lunacies should be laid to rest.

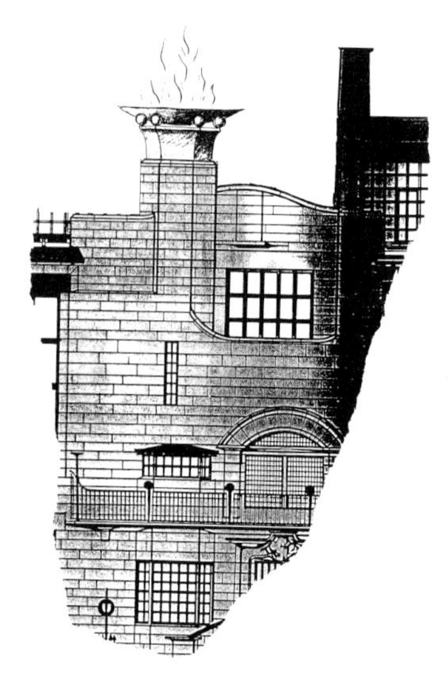

How do you rate his design and layout for the Glasgow School of Art?

The main elevation of the Glasgow School of Art is exceptionally grand and heroic. But that building also explains the whole nature of Mackintosh as a scatterbrain. There's no cohesion in his design, neither outside nor inside, nor between the parts themselves.

As far as planning is concerned, he is conventional and there is no reason to see him as a predecessor of modernism. He just put buildings where he was asked to put them. The School of Art doesn't do anything for the street at all. It was a large enough building to make something significant out of its entrance. Yet the entrance he built is a joke.

He gave his building the scale of a factory with the door of a cottage. This small, mean entrance seems to be like an old building stranded off-centre between two unbalanced bays; three bays of windows on one side and four on the other. As you enter his narrow entrance door you are struck by an immediate conflict of scale, which continues through the whole building. And there are conflicts of materials, too. It's a stone building on the outside, but a very flimsy wooden one on the inside, with too many creaking timbers. I find all this unsatisfactory for a public institution.

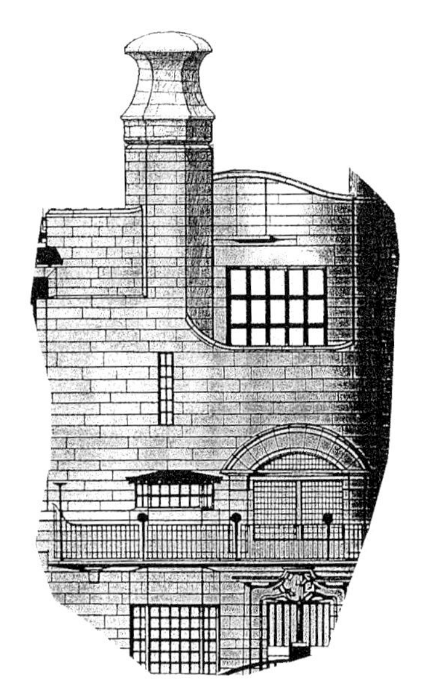

Aldo claims that the School of Art is the world's first non-hierachical in building.

The notion of non-hierarchy in buildings is a misnomer. Buildings have to have a sense of order to function. It's the way people use a building that counts.

What I find objectionable is that the Glasgow School of Art is being held up as a model on how to design today and that Mackintosh is being claimed as one of the fathers of modernism. I find that absolutely outrageous.

Are you saying that the School of Art doesn't look like a public building?

It doesn't really make a public place outside. You walk down the street and it's not better or any worse than any of the other buildings. In Scotland there is a great public awareness of schools being public buildings, more so than in England. You go to any small Scottish village and you immediately know where the school is because it stands out as a strong feature. Mackintosh didn't have a coherent vision of architecture or the way buildings fit into towns. He was more a man of design and detailing.

Would you include his library in the assessment?

I think that's a mess design-wise. The library windows are heroic outside. But the monumental order they establish on the exterior is not carried through to the interior.

So you would agree that what is happening to him today as a kind of stylist is quite reasonable.

Yes, I think he's come into his own in a way. Mackintosh is more a kind of tea shop interior designer than an architect.

Does innovation feature in your value system?

Mackintosh was never asked to do a building requiring innovation. The

BELOW & OPPOSITE
Alternative designs for 'completing' the central tower by Leon Krier.

only justification for innovation is in the creation of new building types such as railway sheds, which never existed before and had to be invented in the nineteenth century. Many architects didn't understand this, so they designed factories in the form of churches and tram sheds like garden gazebos. New building types lead to new types of spans and construction and maybe aesthetics. Historicism in the nineteenth century often meant the misapplication of historical vernaculars which were subsequently misquoted for other uses alien to them, like cathedral-like factories; whereas modernism systematically misquotes the language of technical apparata and misuses it in buildings like Le Corbusier's naval references and the late-industrial quotations Richard Rogers employs in the Pompidou Centre. Mackintosh's work does not misquote from other languages but employs a wild eclecticism of his own. I mean, if you stood in front of one elevation of his art school and were blindfolded and shown another elevation, you would never know it was the same building unless you knew the place. It's that incoherence which postmodernists pick up on, Venturi's extension to the National Gallery, Stirling at the Tate.

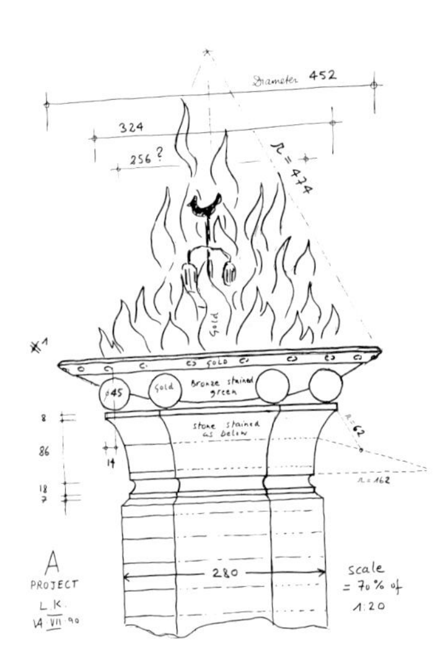

Linlithgow Palace is often given as one possible source of Mackintosh's inspiration from history. Its ashlar walls have large windows on one elevation and small ones on others, but it doesn't appear at all incoherent.

No, that's different. Take Palladio's church of San Giorgio Maggiore in Venice, where the façade is higher than the building itself. It's a symbolic enhancement, like a large stage set, which does not make the building incoherent. But in Mackintosh's school there is nothing apart from the stonework to relate the different façades.

But they face different streets. Given the amount of craft-intensive detailing required it would seem that a good building in your terms would be impossible today.

No, that's not true at all. There are well-crafted buildings being built today using traditional materials. It's not a technical problem of an industrial age to build well. It's a moral problem whether you want to build well and solidly for the future. It's not true that you need an underprivileged under-class to build good buildings.

The problem is that the building industry is now perverted and mostly geared to produce rubbish. Today most of the buildings that look traditional just have a vernacular veneer. This is not to mean that good traditional buildings can't still be built. It's still possible to build using traditional methods and solid wall construction. There's absolutely no technical excuse for building badly.

Do you mean that we should pick up where we left off at some particular moment in history and that the last so many years have been an aberration?

No, it's got nothing to do with history. It's all to do with building techniques. I don't care a damn about oldness or antiquity; it's just that most of what went before was better built and technically superior to what's offered today. You have to take into consideration the projected lifespan of the building and the cost needed for its maintenance. Buildings built well last longer and need fewer repairs. As it is, many buildings are torn down within ten to fifteen years of their construction. Our society predominantly builds rubbish of no lasting importance. I don't care about the past. I just want to return to sound building techniques; they happen to be traditional techniques.

You are not against technological change?

Why should I be? All building techniques have constantly evolved. It's a process of continually adapting, not change for the sake of change. If change is no good it's pointless. The more right you are the less people notice. That's why today there are no heroes of conservation because the more accurately you restore buildings the less people notice. There's no glory in that. You don't get gold medals. You've just done a job well and that's that. Whereas if you go about a building like Scarpa the whole world writes about it. Every idiot can see the difference after Scarpa has worked on an historical building. They think he's great because he has dared to do such things. But the most daring thing you can do to an old building today is to do it right.

Carlo Scarpa. Castelvecchio, Verona, 1963–4. Arrangement of the equestrian statue of Cangrande. Photograph: R Murphy

You don't think very highly of Scarpa?

I think his work is absolutely detestable. For old buildings his influence has been disastrous. All the lunacy that is happening to old buildings in Italy and Spain today is due to Scarpa. Now the conventional thing to do is to rape historical buildings. Innovation has now been institutionalized and written down in the Charter of Venice.

Proposal for Market Tower, Poundbury, for Duchy of Cornwall. Leon Krier, 1991.

So you think Mackintosh was trying to get noticed. Did he have the spirit of an artist rather than an architect?

Yes, that's a profound difference. If you are not in the mainstream of society you have to do something out of the ordinary to get noticed. Now it's getting more and more difficult because Mr Everyman claims loudly to be different and it's getting harder to notice where the differences lie.

So you think that architects should be more like simple artisans than artists?

Yes, absolutely. Just do the job properly. Also I think it's a profession which misguidedly has abandoned its craft base for artistic pretension. Now that the whole world has become deconstructed, it's no longer possible to make a building which stands out.

New College, Oxford, proposed residential buildings; Leon Krier and John Robins, 1990; unsuccessful competition entry.

ALDO VAN EYCK

OPPOSITE
'More beautiful "big" windows that are still windows I have yet to come across.'
Photograph: Glasgow School of Art

WE DECIDED to go north that winter, my wife and I. It was December 1959. I had been working on the orphanage without a break for too long, so we headed for Scotland with the Callanish standing stones as our ultimate destination. The start from Edinburgh's Waverley Station was as good as could be: asking for tickets to Kyle of Lochalsh, the lady in the ticket office exclaimed, 'Dearies, you'll have the islands all to yourselves' – pure poetry, that! On Skye we kept running to avoid cloud breaks between shafts of sunshine for a fortnight, so when finally we got to Glasgow on the way back – nicely tanned – we were well disposed to take in the work of an architect who represents all this and more, and who, reaching for extremes, turned them into exquisite buildings: Mackintosh of course – CRM. I remember climbing that steep slope and, turning into Renfrew Street, being 'struck' by what I saw. Like Michelangelo he accomplished a reconciliation of emotional extremes in architectural terms, thus mitigating inner stress by bringing together formal qualities and aspects deemed incompatible. Struck also by the way CRM, on the threshold of the modern movement, yet still within the nineteenth century, had, taking the past with him into the present without doing it again . . . pointed to the future. Having taken the building in on three sides we passed through what Leon K. calls 'the miserly meanness of the main entrance'. And there was Mr Jefferson Barnes – later the school's director as well as a terrifically nice man, who responded enthusiastically to our enthusiasm. He was one, the very first, to recognize the value of the school (beyond the question of its particular formal style as a period piece) for what it actually is: a superbly well-adjusted environment for art students. CRM reconciled incompatibles by sidestepping all the artificially construed formal barriers and academic categories which still bedevil the architectural

Willow Tea Room facade, 1904. Photograph: Hunterian Art Gallery, University of Glasgow, Mackintosh Collection

scene – blocking the minds of too many architects. He shifted across the familiar panorama of architecture like a true magician, taking with him what we wanted – little – and inventing the rest. An arch non-academician and non-eclectic both. On this rests his modernity – full and early. But it is also why people, like Leon K. and Stanley T., cannot get on with him. Their silly pollutions of the school's incomparable front elevation demonstrated as much.

You were quite damning at the symposium on how art historians have done Mackintosh great injustice.

Indeed I was. Except for the monograph on the Glasgow School of Art (GSA), all the major works on CRM present a biased judgement founded on the erroneous notion that contrary qualities are also incompatible – worlds apart – and to be kept that way. A senseless judgement due to senseless choices – once again it's *or* instead of *and*. In the case of CRM, whose mind and work eludes simplistic categorization and generalization, what is straight, undecorated, geometric and rational has strength, is sound, and is consequently masculine, while what is curved, decorated, organic and emotionally founded is soft and weak and therefore feminine; just think of it! So these authors simply split CRM down the middle. Theirs is a dead-end dialectic – like splitting the alphabet into a set of vowels and a set of consonants in order not to use both within a single word – which would be indeed worse than Welsh, which sounds marvellous! Fixing a gender on to aspects and qualities regarded as contrary is bad enough, but far worse if there is an unwarranted preference for a single direction.

But what if, on top of all this, it is to be taken literally and a real sinner is found, for that is how it is, believe it or not. Had CRM followed his own sound strong and masculine inclinations and resisted the lure of his wife's decorative feminine ways, his stature as precursor, heralding the modern

Van Eyck's drawing of the first floor window of Willow Tea Room, Sauchiehall Street.

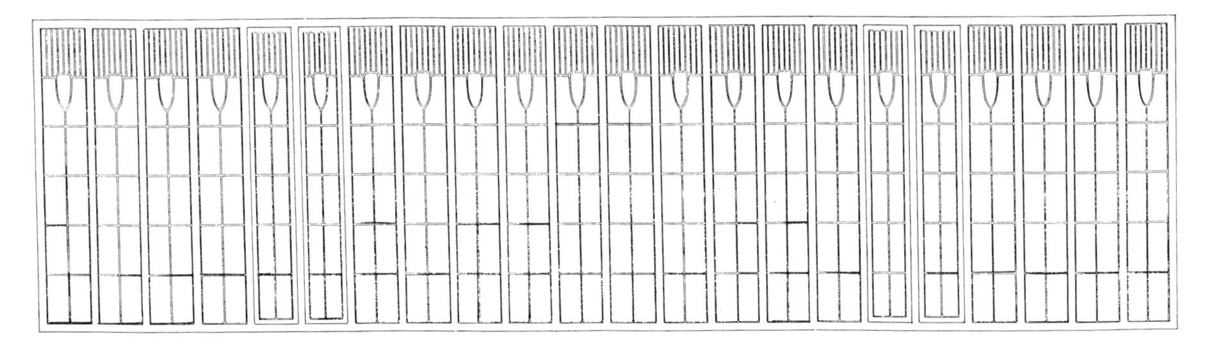

The gallery.
Photograph: Glasgow School of Art

Gallery.
Photograph: T & R Annan & Sons

First floor corridor: west.
Photograph: T & R Annan & Sons

First floor corridor: east.
Photograph: National Monuments
Record of Scotland.

movement, would, they contend, have been greater than it was. How I resent this mental witch-hunt. It is all the more shameful because, lurking behind juxtapositions like straight, curved, strong, weak, and masculine, feminine, there is still the nasty and predictable extension: right – wrong. Without Margaret, CRM would have been a great architect – more purely modern – is their point.

But the truth is quite different: CRM extended the scope of architecture's formal language before it was reduced by the 'moderns' in their search for 'purity'. That he was able to reach beyond the modern movement is due to the very same qualities which, the various authors went out of their way to explain, kept him from becoming one of them – hence 'historically' more important. The irony of it is that his relevance *now* is all the more certain because of these qualities, not in spite of them.

OPPOSITE
Van Eyck's installation *in situ*.
Photograph: Up-front

Take the huge studio windows and the enigmatic brackets slanting inwards towards them. They do not reveal what they'll be like inside against the sky: terrific transmitters of light into studios. More beautiful 'big' windows that are still windows I have never come across. Nor, incidentally, a more appropriately proportioned main entrance through which to slip in and out of an art school than the one located between their windows, the one Leon K. cannot stand.

Did you always know about CRM?

Quite early anyway, but I wasn't 'struck' until that winter. In the CIAM world, remember, people like CRM were forbidden fruit. Team X later turned the same blind eye towards whatever was not flat, plain and pure. 'How are you, Aldo, and how's Mackin*slosh*?', a postcard from the Smithsons enquired. Reactions were similar if I mentioned, say, Horta or Gaudi, Palladio, Romano or Ledoux. Not to mention reference to archaic or tribal architecture.

Over the last twenty-five years appreciations of Mackintosh have advanced from abject neglect to his being embraced as a stylist. While his architecture and spatial contributions still await discovery, 'Mockintosh' decoration has become designer kitsch round town.

There you are: Mockintosh's or Mackinslosh's decoration – but Mackintosh didn't 'decorate' anything. What he did was 'elaborate' – not decorate, and

RETRIEVE WHAT WAS LOST
REPLACE THOSE FIREDOORS
with architecture
way down
in the dumps
there is
no better "school"
for us all

RETRIEVE WHAT WAS LOST
REPLACE THOSE FIREDOORS
with architecture
way down
in the dumps
there is
no better "school"
for us all

all at once
what is there
on either side
is there
SIDE BY SIDE

for the most part locally. These extremely effective elaborations cannot be lifted from where they occur. They are essential and inevitable. Nor is there more of it than is required to 'complete' the story, though without revealing every secret. High-level restraint, I call that. Each elaboration is given its own place, whether square or rose.

Can you expand a little on your perception of Mackintosh's handling of space?

CRM was a true organizer of interior spaces. He composed them in sequence, articulating the latter so as to bring about the right continuity – not too much, nor too little. As you move through the building there is, everywhere, just the right sense of proximity and distance and everything from the smallest to the largest item is just the right size. Spellbound is the word; that's what I was when I went up the school's great central staircase for the first time. Its generous stride and bracing openness take you up with such ease that you want to go down again in order to go up once more. Actually, the same goes for Leon K.'s 'miserly cottage door' through which I had just passed. It makes you want to enter and re-enter again and again, which is as it should be, surely.

OPPOSITE
Van Eyck's drawing of installation.

You highlighted a telling detail from a Mackintosh tea room in your GSA installation.

You mean those little mirrors set in plain glass right across the tea room façade along Sauchiehall Street. Yes, indeed, I have expanded on that particular 'elaboration' no end of time over the years, always using the photograph I made on that first occasion. So I did once again for my little installation for the GSA exhibition.

Thanks to these mirrors what is there on either side is all at once there side by side: I mean – exterior and interior – street and room (city and building) – large and small – all simultaneously present as they are held within the surface of that window.

As for the little 'Tea Room' window I installed in the GSA, it opened on to another – different – 'street' in the school's interior. It brings to mind what was lost when the fire doors appeared later on every floor.

CRM, you see, knew what art is all about, what the prerogatives are; thus also what the *pulse* of an art school should be. So what he came up with

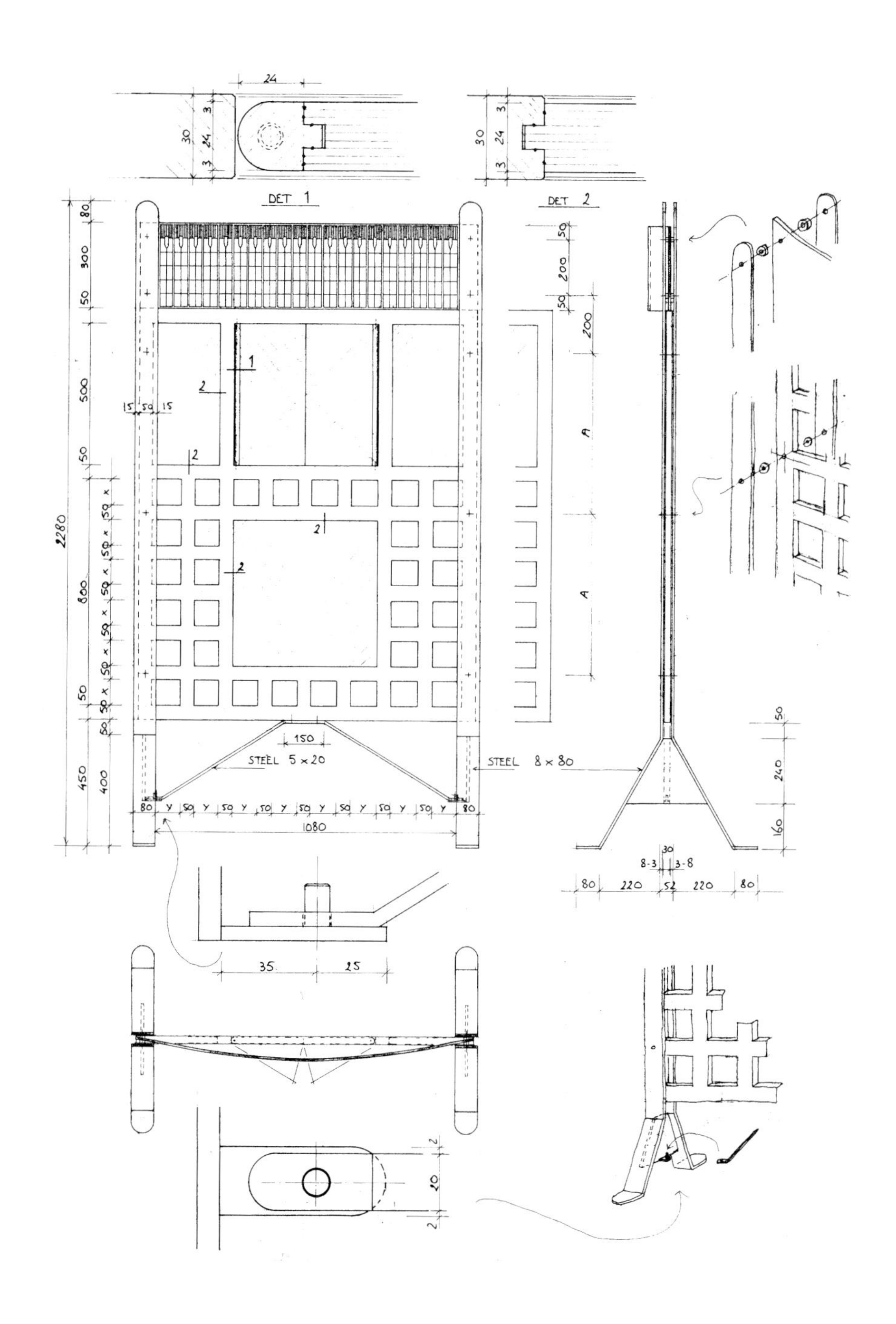
DET 1
DET 2
STEEL 5 × 20
STEEL 8 × 80
2280
1080
150
35
25

next to so much else, was certainly no corridors, but streets with *interior urbanity* along which the school's various localities are gathered and all and sundry occurs.

The generosity and warmth of this great unifying device (with miraculous staircases playing their part) is unique and surely CRM's most revolutionary and enduring single gesture (another opportunity never came his way). But also his most intrinsically 'modern' one in that the stigma of authority is absent and nothing hierarchical is sensed. A core for people 'multilateral' in spirit.

Proposal: – Retrieve what was lost, so the 'streets' will be there again
– Replace the fire doors!
– Do so step by step – floor by floor, the inner ones first. Thus, at each stage – as the streets open up – there will be every reason for celebration.
– And remember: he was a master in the use of 'iron', glass and transparency. So there's your cue. As for the new doors: they must remain open unless emergency requires them closed.

GSA is a gentle building if ever there was one – its strength lies in its generosity. There is also no school more spirited. In fact, with architecture way down in the dumps, *there is no better 'school' for us all*. Nor was there ever a better architect – that's saying an awful lot, but it's all right: he shares that tribute with others, though not that many.

How on earth did he do it? Or, what brought about a building which was not equal when it comes to the way each window and each door – each bit of wood, stone, iron or glass – each tile (and every rosebud) – every place and every dimension whomever it accommodates must be the better for it – and gratefully bewildered.

Leon Krier was critical of the school's small entrance, which signalled for him that it was a private not a public building.

Critical is not the right word. He simply demonstrated physical distaste of the building, which is telling us something about Leon K.'s private self but nothing about the building. However, his black ill-humoured intervention pointed to the current semi-professional malady I call RPP (Rats, Posts and other Pests). And so did Stanley T., author of that other exterior pollution which was just as black and silly as Leon K.'s.

The school happened to be the subject of renewed assessment – hence also scrutiny, so its exterior disfigurement was, on that score alone, a gross impropriety. Only temporary, it was argued, but the mental scar is not. Stanley T. calls what he did 'only plastic surgery', which turned out to be just another self-portrait nobody wants. The GSA is wasted on despoilers of this sort. I questioned whether I should contribute at all, in that particular building, with them around, you remember. Sometimes two divergent levels should be kept apart.

Do you think Mackintosh is inescapably Scottish?

I was waiting for that! The Dutch, you know, never stop highlighting Mondrian's Dutchness (he himself soon gave up spelling his name the Dutch way, with a double a). The truth is that Holland looks more like Mondrian than Mondrian like Holland. The same goes for CRM's Scottishness. Although, I suppose, as an outsider, I do associate him with Scotland, but not with a Celtic emphasis. None the less, he is a 'twilight' architect if ever there was one. Twilight standing for day and night; the way an eclipse stands for sun and moon and what they in turn stand for. Mackintosh was close to all that, so he took it in his stride – the entire panorama – the full panorama.

Mother's Home, Amsterdam by Aldo van Eyck. Photograph: Courtesy of Aldo van Eyck.

Has Mackintosh informed your own work?

Something would be amiss if he hadn't. Fabulous architecture, where and whenever, is mental nourishment – but that goes for fabulous art in general. I was aware of CRM's presence during the final stage of the orphanage; it was approaching completion at the time. From the start, I wanted a non-hierarchical configuration of spaces strung along an articulated interior street. The GSA was therefore an encouraging confirmation of what I had done. What if I'd seen the GSA a few years earlier? Well, that would have done no harm! Since CRM's personal touch is intoxicating, I tried to keep clear of it (bar a few lamps!). In fact, I always resist reacting directly in architectural terms to strong formal impact; though of course, not the meaning or message it may convey.

Why do you think Mackintosh ran out of commissions?

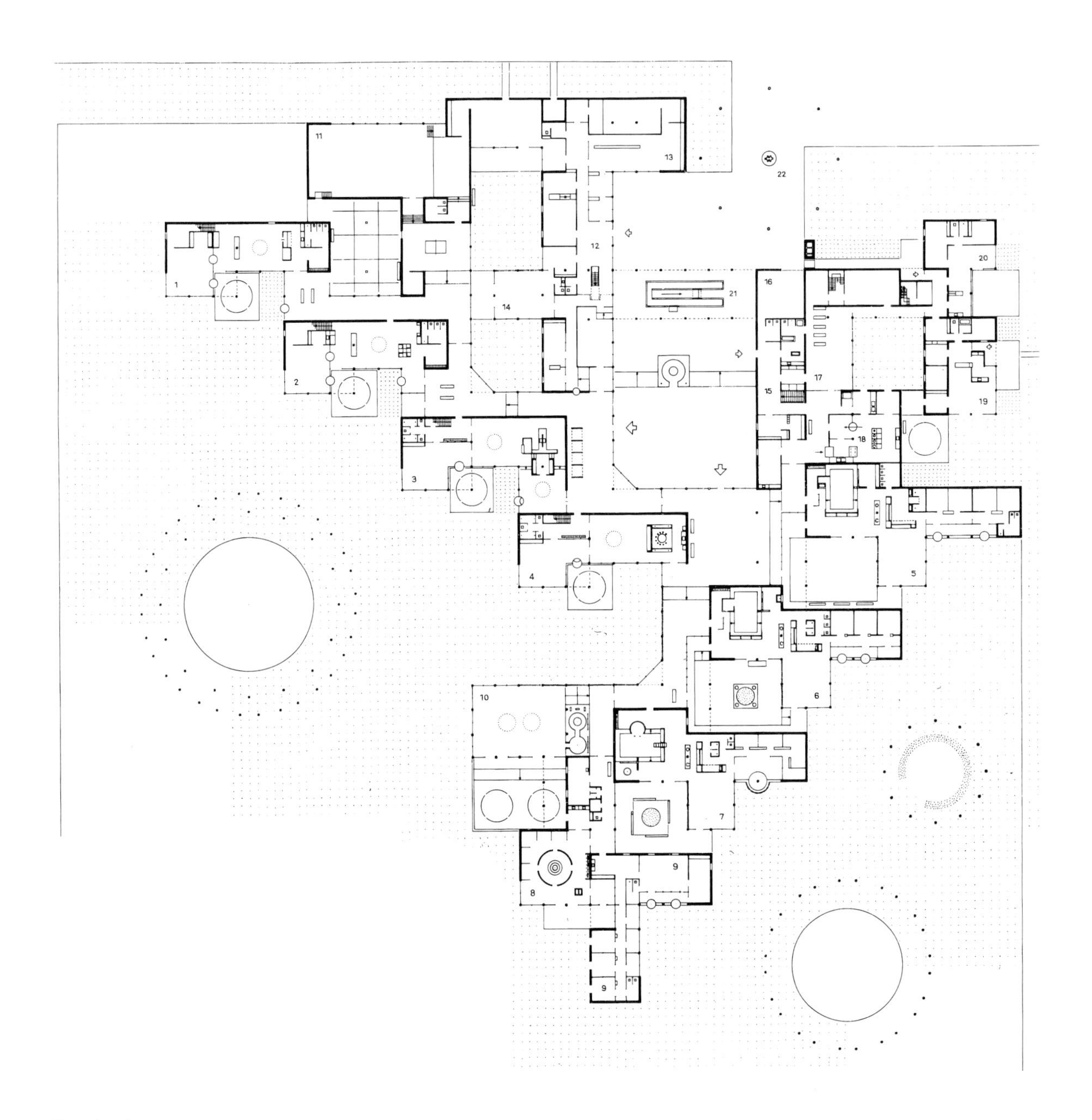

Plan of orphanage.

He was simply too good at it – and to fall in line or go along with one like him is not everybody's ability or choice. Your question stings a bit. Since the Scots and Dutch are not quite the same, there must have been another reason why I, incidentally, was not asked to build more than I have. Not a single public building ever came my way – let alone on a site it could easily have spoilt – until recently, when a small art centre did on just such a site!

Is there anything more you would like to add?

Architects are there to render service. To do otherwise consciously is nothing less than treason – intellectual cowardice. I refer to the cynicism with which this era's great avant garde in art and science is currently being ridiculed by the RPP. And thus CRM, who anticipated so much more than the architects of the modern movement's second generation were prepared to absorb. CRM took the lonesome road in the opposite direction to that of today's regressive spoilsports. He is still far ahead.

Finally: what he did could not have been done without lots of encouragement and intelligent criticism; not if the buildings were to be good ones, and they were very, very good.

So here's to Margaret, who stood by her husband so long and so well, playing her part in what is surely a miraculous achievement.

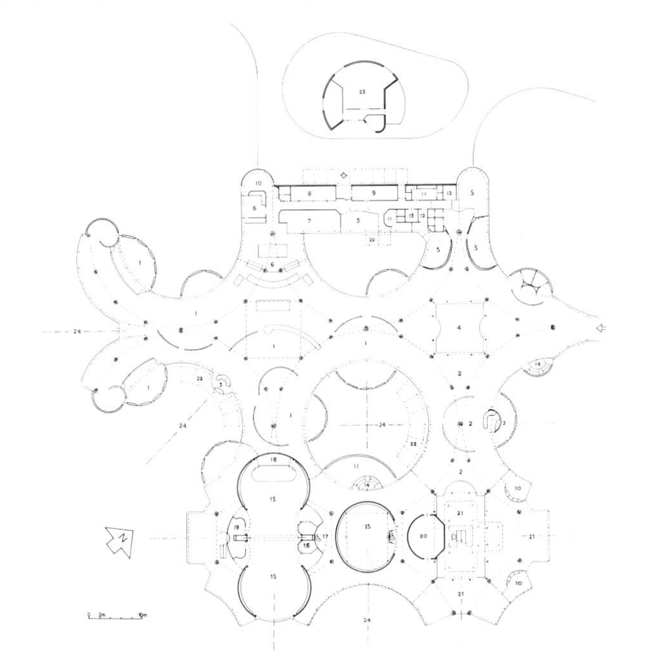

Plan of ESTEC Centre.

STANLEY TIGERMAN

GIVEN THAT THIS amazing icon was built in two stages specifically and given that Mackintosh's production reached its maturity in the age of 'arts and crafts' generally, his ambivalence about asymmetry is understandable. Our project is to address (or 'correct') this ambivalence by 'healing' Mackintosh's doubt about the conjunction of the phases in this project (to say nothing about his 'doubt' about the two pressures informing his career – the literal historicism inferred by his fascination with the Romanesque, versus his concern with the abstraction of the grid). Black grids are utilized in order to 're-centre' the school by tracing over the asymmetric constellation of architectural elements Mackintosh used to concentrate the entrance façade in order to ennoble the building's entrance.

A footnote: It seemed appropriate, finally to re-consider Leon Krier's signature proposal in much the same way . . . this is only plastic surgery, after all.

Decoration of Scotland Street School.
Photograph: Glasgow School of Art

Can you give us your initial reactions to the School of Art?

As you know, the conference was the second time I had visited Glasgow. The first was to see the Mackintosh School of Art specifically, to get a sense of where and what I might do as an installation. I thought that the School of Art was absolutely brilliant in its simplicity, combined with what detail that Mackintosh could get away with (he was clearly a practical man, as one observes on the spartan rear elevation). The central space of that old building is noble without relying on classical precedent, and the studios are as useful now as they were originally, I'm sure. It's just too bad that the additions and new buildings over the years are so grim, and just basically mean. It's almost

OPPOSITE
Stanley Tigerman's installation in the centre of the School of Art. (The flame on the top of the tower is an approximate realisation of Leon Krier's proposals.)
Photograph: Courtesy of Stanley Tigerman

biblically just that the architects and planners work in the mean-spirited newer buildings, and the painters and sculptors still have access to the best in building. Poor Andy MacMillan, it's his destiny, I guess!

As the sole American contributor to the exhibition and symposium, can you tell us of your understanding of Mackintosh from an American context. Is his architectural contribution understood there, or is he seen merely as a furniture designer?

After spending some considerable time in and around Glasgow observing much of his work (the Art School, The Hill House, Queen's Cross Church, the Willow restaurant, the reconstruction at the museum, etc.), my considered view that the American perception of Mackintosh as primarily an interior designer, as well as a designer of eccentrically beautiful objects is, for me at least, sustained. His architectural contributions are quirky and not particuarly consistent – but then look at the quirkiness, architecturally speaking, of Glasgow's architecture. He is a perfect fit in a city whose inconsistent urban plan is mollified somewhat by its individual architectural virtuoso efforts. The more ornate aspects of Mackintosh's decorative work bear some relationship to Louis Sullivan's ornamentation drawn from nature, but the omniscient gridding that has captivated American architects and designers is, after all, equally present in the work of Josef Hoffmann. Now, while it is true that all these gentlemen were nominally contemporaries, Mackintosh is a bit of a late-comer. Make no mistake, I admire Mackintosh almost (but not quite) as much as the fuss that is made of him in Glasgow. If I, for one, were a Glaswegian, I would share some of the spotlight with 'Greek' Thomson, who is much more interesting architecturally than Mackintosh.

Louis Sullivan. Detail Prudential Building, Chicago, 1894. Photograph: CRM Society library

In your contribution to the exhibition you talked about the conversation between symmetry and asymmetry; you tried to 'correct' the middle of the front façade. Can you expand on what you meant by that gesture?

History tells us that Mackintosh built the art school in two stages, which makes the eccentricity of the centralized entrance that much more palpable. What I tried to accomplish in my intervention was to conduct a dialogue with the building on the subject of symmetry versus asymmetry, relying on the gridded aspect of Mackintosh's work as the conduit of the dialogue. Thus, for every eccentric element (window, ornament, etc.) that he incorporated at the (new) centre of the building in its final stage, I showed the 'trace' of that

Gridded metal work at the head of the stair tower. Photograph: Keith Gibson

element in a gridding in a location about the centre line of the completed building.

You described Mackintosh as an 'in-between' architect: between nineteenth and twentieth centuries; between literalism and abstraction. This suggests either a kind of schizophrenia or perhaps a sense of hesitation in the face of the twentieth century. How do you read his place at this point in history?

I read Mackintosh's 'place' in the history of architecture located as it was in that strange time between the failure of Arts and Crafts to make a transition from literal classicism *and* the Victorian age, to the no-nonsense, stripped-down early modernism of the second decade of this century. Mackintosh, and numerous others like him in Austria, England and the United States, were caught in a time in between times, and their work both benefits and suffers from that uneasy location. Of course, there was an ambivalence – one can only imagine what it must have been like having both the former and the latter peering at those who were uncertain about where society was going politically, culturally, etc. Much has been written on the subject, but in Mackintosh's case, at least, it's clear that he was stretched thin between epochs that bracketed his own; and it's also clear that when the brave new world came at last, he was not particularly prepared for it and his career dwindled down, sadly enough, and he went out more with a T.S. Eliot whimper than anything else.

You were particularly excited by what you described as the 'grid' in his work; it's seen as an organizing mechanism and a scale-giver; and yet other contributors saw these assemblies of squares to do with the perforation of surface. Can you comment?

I would personally prefer that the grid perforate van Eyck's brain, myself. Seriously, I believe that Mackintosh's grid is both an abstraction (grids always are) and can also be read as a way to make his work accessible through measurement (once you know the size of one of the grids you know them all, and you therefore come to know the 'size' of what the grids denominate). Far less personal than Mackintosh's use of post-romanesque ornamentation, each one none the less represents one of the two poles between which Mackintosh's work is situated.

Tigerman's installation: axonometric and elevation.

Do you see any similarities between your own work and that of Mackintosh, or have your visits to Glasgow affected your current work in any way?

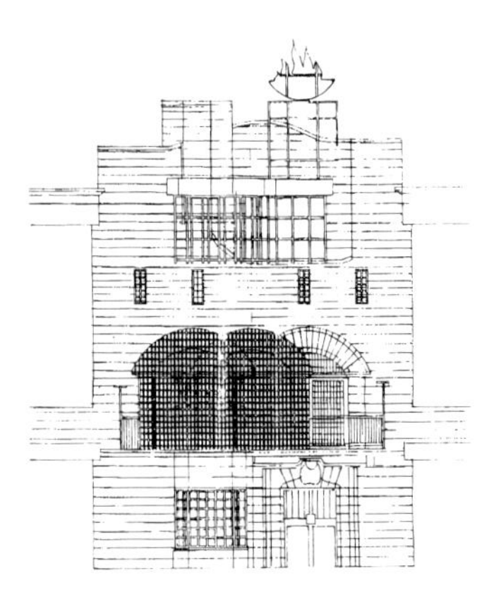

The part of Mackintosh's work that has always fascinated me is the 'grid' but then, I have the same fascination with Hoffmann and others equally persuaded to 'mark' their work with the trace of measurement not found in their own use of material repetitiously driven (brick, concrete block, etc.). The side of Mackintosh's work that interests me only as a voyeur is his use of Art Nouveau decoration. It is far too personal to have any paradigmatic value in the larger analysis of nineteenth- and twentieth-century evolution, and can only be admired, in my view, as a 'one-off' idiosyncratic production.

I feel that my own work neither benefits nor suffers from my trips to Glasgow. But then, I am not particularly influenced by 'travel'. The larger issues of the day in the United States are far more consequential for me than to be too taken by the picturesqueness of earlier times. The potential that is located between architecture and homelessness, AIDS, and America's underclass generally, is more poignant in its possibilities than to seek

validation by precedent (and, in the case of Mackintosh, a precedent that is best described as 'peculiar'). Which is not to say that I am not struck by Mackintosh's singular inability to 'cope' with the issues of his own transitional times. He is a figure among many of his day who did not really know what to make of the changing times and their political, social and ultimately architectural manifestations. My heart goes out to him, I suppose, but then my heart goes out to all those who are uncertain – and vulnerable – to a mechanism of society with which they cannot cope.

Momochi District. Housing Complex, Fukuoka, Japan, 1988/89. Stanley Tigerman.
Photograph: Courtesy of Stanley Tigerman

HANS HOLLEIN

ALONG WITH A small group of architecture students, I knew about Mackintosh, not so much from his connection with the Vienna Werkstätte, as from reading about the Glasgow School of Art as one of the key buildings in the early modern movement. Our knowledge of this was all self-gathered, since neither Mackintosh nor any of the Viennese architects such as Otto Wagner, Josef Hoffmann and Adolf Loos were taught at the academy then.

When I studied Hoffmann he was still alive, but few people knew of him or his importance. I remember when Alvar Aalto came as one of the Vienna Centre prizewinners, he spent most of his time talking to Hoffmann. The building-department people looked aghast and had no idea who the old man was or what he had done.

I was just flabbergasted in the 1950s concerning how little was known about the Viennese architects Loos, Wagner and Hoffmann; almost nobody had heard of Klimt. Now Vienna is plastered full of false images of Klimt. When I was a student I could have bought Klimt drawings for £5 and Hoffmann chairs could be found in attics for nothing. I remember mounting a big attack on our museum of applied arts at a time when they were extending their Meissen china collection and neglecting their duty to collect works from their own specific culture. All they said was, 'We have no money.' In fact, they could have acquired Hoffmann furniture for ridiculously low amounts, but preferred to do nothing. I remember that America was the same, except for Frank Lloyd Wright. Shortly before his death, Wright invited me to Taliesin, Wisconsin, and was elated that I recognized his Klimt painting.

The interesting thing about the situation in Vienna (I don't know how it was in Scotland) was that architects, not art historians, were researching

'A creator of shifting experiences as you move through his buildings.' Bedford Lemere.
Photograph: Glasgow School of Art

OPPOSITE
'We saw his tea-rooms not so much as decoration as the creation of atmospheric spaces.'
Photograph: Hunterian Art Gallery, University of Glasgow, Mackintosh Collection

'I feel Mackintosh knew unconsciously about agoraphobia and claustrophobia.'
(The Hill House, Helensburgh, 1902–3) Living room.
Photograph: Glasgow School of Art

Hollein's exhibits in the library, Glasgow School of Art.
Photograph: Up-front

the work of people like Loos, Hoffmann and Wagner. Historians weren't interested at all. We would have to wait for the next generation for that. As architects, we knew about Mackintosh's music room in Vienna, but it was impossible for a few architects like ourselves to spend a year of creative time just researching.

It was the same in Glasgow. The Ingram Street Tea Rooms were saved by Glasgow's Planning Department, not by the art and museum people. The city art gallery never mentioned Mackintosh until the late 1960s. Did you understand Mackintosh instantly as a precursor of modernism?

OPPOSITE
'He had an understanding of how books can engulf you in study.'
Photograph: National Monuments Record of Scotland

Absolutely, yes. I think the Vienna movement was sympathetic towards Mackintosh because he never separated the outside from the inside. He made no distinction between architecture and interior design that was so fashionable in the United States. Mackintosh was welcomed in Vienna because he had also no bias against doing small-scale work and designed furniture down to the smallest exquisite detail. Of course, we all had the strong interest in the non-quantitative aspect of Mackintosh's work, in the way he created atmosphere within a building. We saw his tea rooms not so much as decoration as the creation of atmospheric spaces.

When did you first visit Glasgow?

I saw Murray's film on Mackintosh at the Venice Biennale in the late 1960s. It conveyed a real coherence of spatial atmosphere and the sense of Mackintosh's complexities of three-dimensionality, which was quite different from the string of nice pictures that make up most architecture films. It was a good prelude for my first visit to the Glasgow School of Art in 1972. I was immediately impressed. It was extremely modern and avant-garde, yet at the same time had a strong relationship with Scottish heritage. Unlike most of the other modernist buildings, which consciously created a gap between their locally specific past, Mackintosh's Glasgow School of Art was exceptional, though the interesting heterogeneity of the building was considered in those days as completely incoherent. The two side façades spoke two different languages. Big studio windows were asymmetrically positioned either side of a traditional entrance. There was an intense play between the large-scale and the small-scale, all beautifully detailed.

But the exquisite handling of materials is part of the craft of any good

Haas House, Stefansplatz, Vienna.
Photograph: Courtesy of Hans
Hollein.

'I did not try to make one coherent facade. I tried to make one coherent whole.'

architect and should be taken for granted. I think Mackintosh has since suffered the fate that people admire his little skills and his water-colours. To me this was only confirmation that here was a great man, a great artist, but what was really interesting went beyond all this. Mackintosh brought into architecture a determined complexity which he handled masterfully. There are many buildings which suddenly get complex because the architect doesn't know how to handle a lot of unresolved problems. With Mackintosh, there is a complexity of thought, of architectural possibilities and architectural elements. He was a master of circulation, not in a functional sense like a factory, where something comes in and goes out as a product, but as a creator of shifting experiences as you move through his buildings. A building, in Mackintosh's hands, ceases to be corridors and stairs, but offers moments of discovery, of exciting spatial experiences such as when you come into and walk through the 'hen run' in Glasgow School of Art. Mackintosh offers us an experience of understanding how life in such a building could be.

Would you agree with Aldo that it's an anti-authoritarian building?

Yes, it is an anti-authoritarian building, just as Scottish castles are non-authoritarian buildings, even though they emanate a strong force of power. This may be because they have a slight touch of romanticism. I think Mackintosh was also a very romantic architect.

This might have allowed him to draw on a synthesis of elements from the Scottish vernacular to the Japanese?

I think Mackintosh, like many of the Vienna architects, admired the Japanese approach to decoration because it was completely different from classicism. They set about transferring the same refinement of surface and colour into their work.

Warndorfer Salon (Music room), Vienna, *c.*1902, by C R Mackintosh. Photograph: Hunterian Art Gallery, University of Glasgow, Mackintosh Collection

Why do you think there's been a reawakening of interest in Mackintosh's work today? You have mentioned complexity, relationship to space and romanticism. Are those all issues you think are interesting to architects today?

Well, I think what is really interesting is not all those separate aspects but Mackintosh's capacity to handle many different aspects and shape them all into a complex and superior whole. One sees this in the work of Scarpa, too. Architecture is no longer a fight between reactionary and modernist tendencies. Most modern architects can create a passable building, one that is not at all bad, that handles all the formulas competently. These buildings seldom end in disasters but then they are not of high quality either. Mackintosh allows his buildings to cater to a lot of differentiated demands. He is able to satisfy the inner psychological demands of human beings. That's what is interesting. But how can you instil these qualities into a building today using everyday production techniques? I must confess that I don't quite have the answer to that.

I think what interests architects today in Mackintosh is how he achieved the feelings you get as you move through his interiors. For me it's more about making a statement than solving a problem. I don't think a building is a solution to a problem. Even so, Le Corbusier once said that the problem well stated is almost the solution. I think good architecture goes far beyond the solution to a problem when it enters the realms of the psychological. As an architect you are not standing in front of any empty canvas and saying, *Look, I have a problem to solve here.* You make a statement. And so Mackintosh had to make his statement.

When training, you learn about architecture *from* architecture. You learn certain rules and you progress from building to building. I feel that Mackintosh drew on other sources. I think he understood a lot about the psychology of space. I feel Mackintosh knew unconsciously about claustrophobia and agoraphobia. Space-making is the stuff of great architecture but it's never on a school curriculum. Mackintosh intuited what his clients would need. What's interesting is that normally a client gives you a brief about his needs. They are very much concerned with small, little practical things which are of course important. Two bathrooms, a toilet and the size of the kitchen, separate bedrooms etc., but the non-quantitative aspects are never written down. When you want to build a *home*, not a house, you have completely

Aircraft carrier in the landscape. Project 1964. Collection MOMA, New York.
Photograph: Courtesy of Hans Hollein

different things in mind. Two people are unable to articulate these because there is no real language to convey such subtleties. Or if there is, they don't dare articulate this 'extrovertness' or 'introvertness'. But these are the really interesting things which make a home and which Mackintosh, unasked for, delivered at The Hill House for Blackie.

It's hard to connect the requirements of the brief with what Mackintosh ultimately delivered in the library of the Glasgow School of Art.

Yes, sure, I think he had an understanding of how books can engulf you in study. Mackintosh created this library as a retreat, not just a space to pick up some quick information out of a book. Here there is a profound understanding about the relationship between man and knowledge.

This was where you placed your installation.

Here I wanted to distil the sum of what I thought were the important notions in Mackintosh's work. I wanted to convey certain tendencies in Mackintosh's vocabulary. One of these was the squared grid, which he transcended in the Glasgow School of Art by giving it such a great complexity of meanings.

Of course this concern with the square was a bridge to Vienna, especially to Hoffmann. Whoever was the first with this is a moot question, but it certainly provided a convivial exchange of ideas at the turn of the century. The two tendencies of the geometrical and the natural pervade Mackintosh's work, and I wanted to show this in my exhibit.

Originally I wanted to delineate a number of themes that Mackintosh pursued in his architecture by gilding different parts of the exterior of the School of Art. As this proved a little difficult, I decided on a more abstract scheme by flying a series of banners in the library. Mackintosh's attitude to the 'modern' is exemplified in the grid. His work also combines a medieval or gothic strain with a more floral form of expression. So I devised a series of transformations. A basic gridded square; an oblique grid; a curved and wavy one; a gothic and monumental one and finally a playful one. These transformations represent tendencies in Mackintosh's work which I find relevant to contemporary architecture.

I became very interested in these different aspects when I did the Haas Haus in Vienna, opposite the cathedral. Like the art school, this building has consciously different façades. I did not try to make one coherent façade.

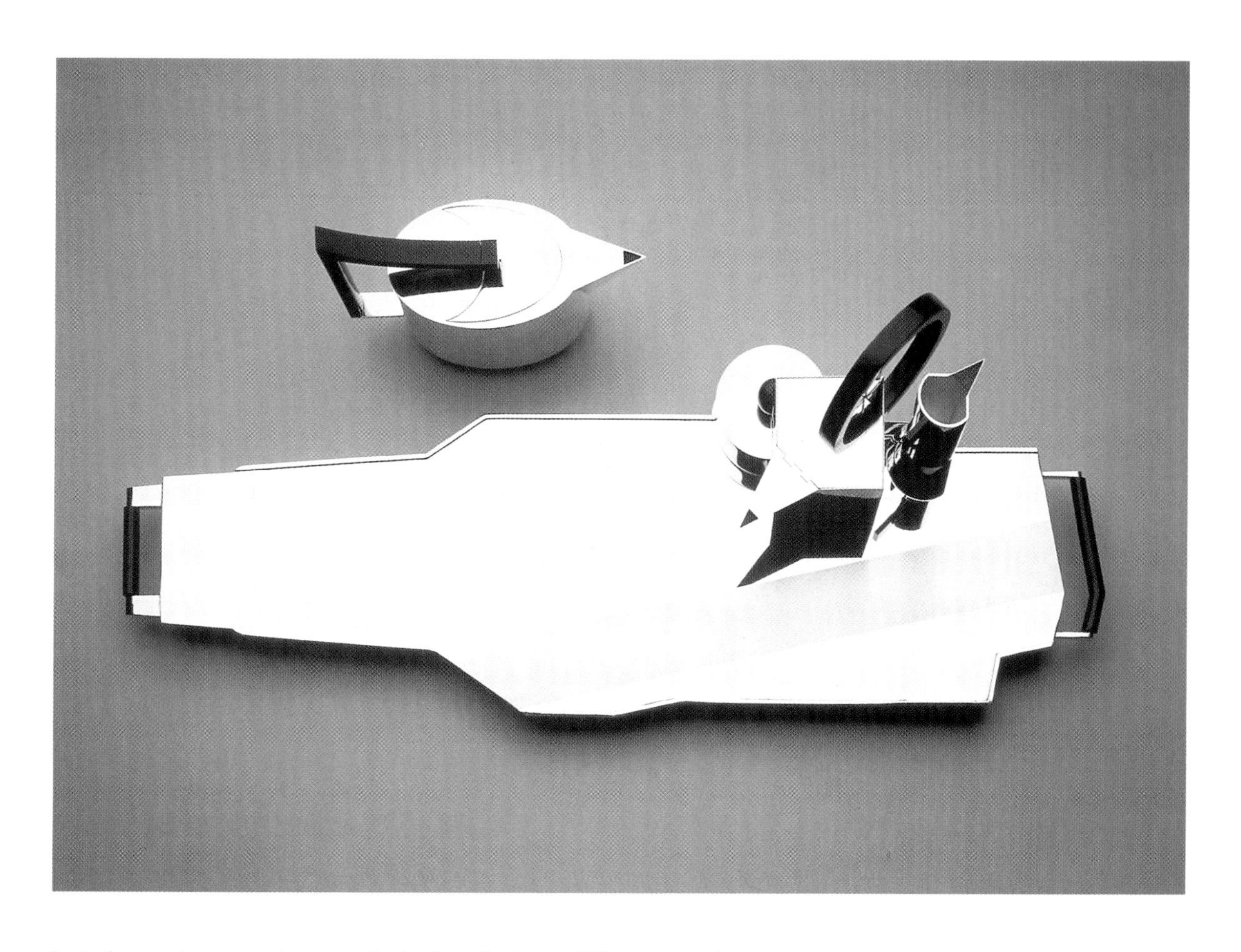

Aircraft carrier tea and coffee set for Alessi Italy, 1980.

I tried to make one coherent whole. I made these different façades speak different languages. The curved one followed the buildings that were already there, which were simply walls punched with holes. But unlike them, I didn't want this façade to have a tectonic appearance of one stone piled on another. So I used a diagonally-cut stone facing to give the effect of a membrane, what Philip Johnson aptly calls wallpaper. The next façade is a modern part with glass and aluminium with a cantilever jutting out. But to face the cathedral and the medieval streets I created what I call a 'gothic' façade. Of course, this has nothing to do with pointed arches but is in the same spirit I perceived in certain aspects of Mackintosh's work.

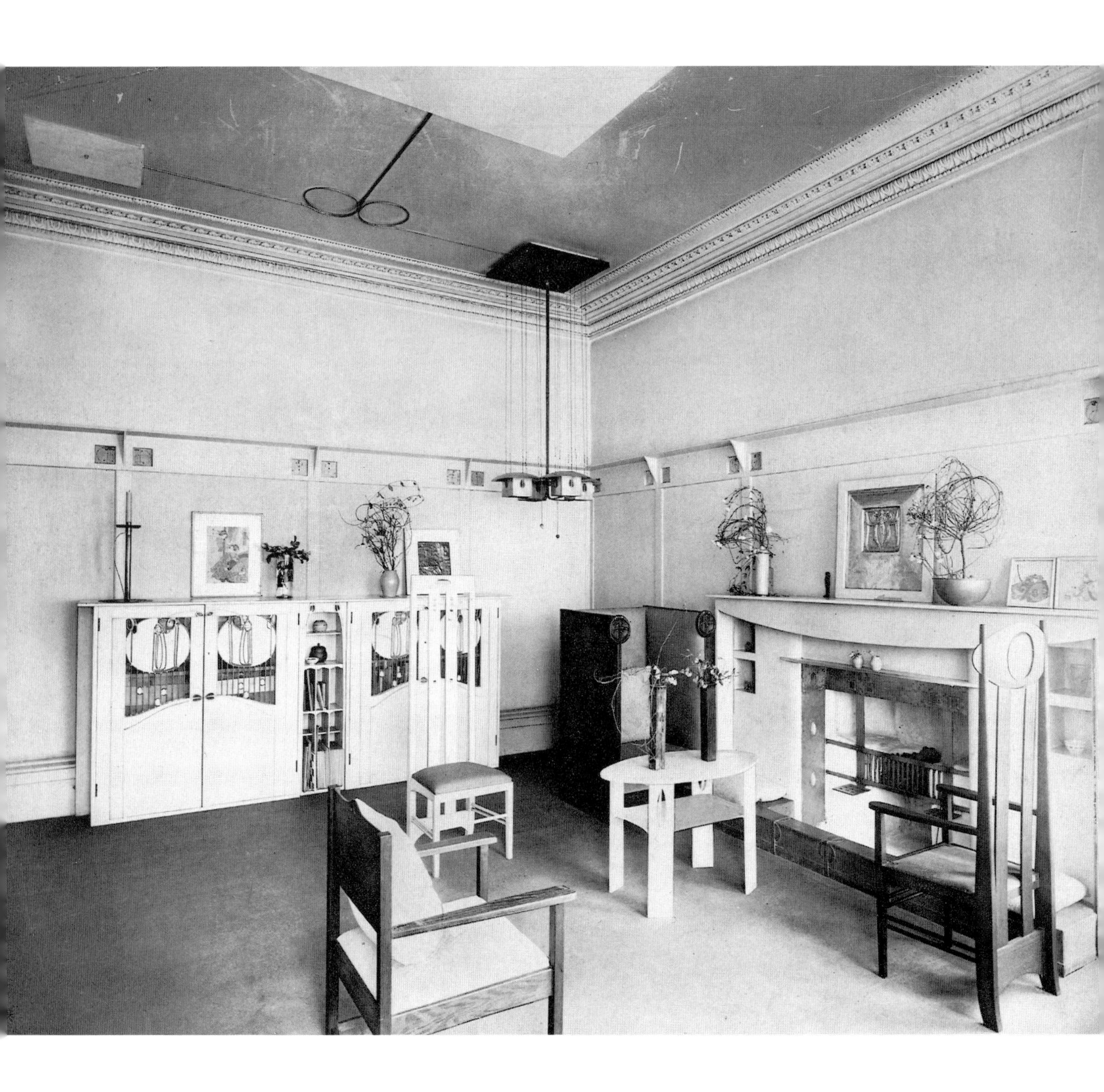

ARATA ISOZAKI

A Japanese person looking at the work of Charles Rennie Mackintosh is immediately struck by how very 'Japanese' his designs are. The simplicity needs no explanation. It is amazing how he has grasped the essence of Japanese aesthetics.

On my first visit to Glasgow in 1970 I hoped to discover how such a unique aesthetic had been nurtured in a place so far, both geographically and culturally, from Japan. But a tour of Mackintosh's Glasgow work only deepened my confusion. Granted, the exterior surface decoration of his Glasgow buildings and much of his furniture was singularly flat, but the buildings themselves were, to my Japanese sensibilities, sturdy stone edifices moulded like sculpture.

The seeming contradiction, I realize, originates more in myself than in Mackintosh's work, for I am looking at these structures through twentieth-century eyes conditioned to soaring steel girders and transparent glass surfaces. Mackintosh's novel juxtaposition of sculptural structure and flat surface ornamentation gave me much food for thought and was to affect my own work thereafter.

Mackintosh arrived on the architectural scene when Japanese-inspired Impressionism was at its peak and Art Nouveau was just emerging. Manet and Van Gogh were imitating Japanese woodblock prints. Emile Zola and Stephane Mallarmé were avidly collecting things Japanese, and a Japanese painter was working as a designer in the atelier of the Nancy school. Out of these trends evolved an expressive technique of flat planes devoid of shadows.

For centuries the dominant pictorial style in Europe had been one in which illusionary techniques were used to give flat objects three-dimensional contours. In the late nineteenth century, the shadows were abandoned as the

Mackintosh's student lodgings, showing furniture and mural. Note Japanese prints above fireplace. Photograph: Hunterian Art Gallery, University of Glasgow, Mackintosh Collection

OPPOSITE
The Mackintoshes' apartment: more Japanese prints left. Photograph: Hunterian Art Gallery, University of Glasgow, Mackintosh Collection

OPPOSITE
Arata Isozaki's installation of chairs, jointly inspired by Marilyn Monroe and Mackintosh, in the top studio with Japanese inspired roof carpentry.
Photograph: Up-front

emphasis shifted to flat, two-dimensional colour and line rather than three-dimensional illusion. Much later, Cubists and Futurists would create a whole new dimension by introducing the abstract elements of space and time. Mackintosh's kind of flat Japanese aesthetic filled the transitional void between traditional and contemporary architectural aesthetics.

I do not have the resources at this point to explain in detail how a trend emerging out of Paris took hold in a place like Glasgow. What I do know is that Charles Rennie Mackintosh certainly must have felt some kind of affinity with the Japanesque trend. At the very least, he must have been familiar with the preceding Chinese influences that entered into Europe. Chinoiserie was highly popular in eighteenth-century England, when numerous pieces of lacquered Ming furniture were imported into Europe. Mackintosh must have seen for himself these imports with their combination of straight and subtly curved lines. The Japanese objects that were imported later were notable for their functionality, having been made as they were by a people with little comprehension of decoration for decoration's sake. Those Japanese paintings that did make their way into Europe at the turn of the century were for the most part peaceful depictions of nature – for example of seasonal flowers and birds – meant to calm the mind and fill the heart with repose. Dramatic, combative painting was so rare as to be almost non-existent.

The same room.
Photograph: Studio Brett

Art Nouveau is not my speciality, but I have often wondered if the organic line of the genre represents a re-emergence of ancient Celtic motifs. If this were so, it makes it easier to understand why Mackintosh and his contemporaries in Glasgow chose bold, flat floral motifs to decorate the inner surfaces of their architecture.

When I embarked upon my 1970 trip to view Mackintosh's work, there was very little published about him in Japan. The colour pictures I photographed on that trip were for a long time the only printable pictures of his work in Japan and for a decade or so, my photos were in great demand among Japanese publishers. This was the first, and last, time I performed the function of architectural photographer.

The apparently contradictory external architectural style and inner decoration of Mackintosh's work confused me only because I am a product of later, contemporary architectural styles distinguished by their lack of sculptural elements and flat structural compositions. I encountered Mackintosh just when my dissatisfaction with modern architecture was

bubbling to the surface. Modern architecture, it seemed to me, had sacrificed much in its single-minded pursuit of principle. In contrast Mackintosh stood at an intermediate point between Western and Celtic and pre-Raphaelite trends and imported Japanesque tendencies; between organized Art Nouveau and geometric Art Deco. In his work I discovered an important element, an element modern architecture has lost.

Since 1970 I have been exploring techniques of spatial construction that come closer to the geometric three-dimensional construction traditional to the West, than to the forced fusion of flat planes that is the traditional Japanese approach to architecture. My search is at once a criticism of traditional Japanese architectural technique and a carry-on, I believe, of Mackintosh's own quest. In this pursuit I have flattened my surfaces, interjecting within the resulting space sometimes sculptural elements, sometimes geometric contours.

OPPOSITE
Aska Houses by Arata Isozaki, 1974–88.
Living room.
Photograph: Yukio Futagawa

Back in the mid-1960s when I first began working independently, I happened to make a template of French curves based on the physical contours of Marilyn Monroe. I took these curves from nude calendar photos of Marilyn Monroe that had been taken when she was still an unknown. I made repeated attempts to construct a chair using this template but could never produce anything satisfactory. Later, when I visited the Glasgow School of Art, I saw cabinets and chairs designed by Mackintosh in the high-back style that seems to have been popular at the time. Frank Lloyd Wright made sketches of a similar kind of chair at the beginning of this century. I decided to try adapting this style of chair to my Marilyn Monroe curves and succeeded in 1974 in making a prototype. This particular piece now belongs to the Kita-Kyushu Municipal Museum of Art.

Mackintosh is said to have designed several dozens of pieces of furniture in a single night. It took me ten years to make a single chair. First I had to make my template of curves, then I had to make a paper pattern, next I made a metal model, and so on and so forth. The effort was so exhausting I have never attempted another chair since.

If Marilyn Monroe was my muse in the 1950s of my youth, then Charles Rennie Mackintosh was one of my most important teachers in the 1960s. My chair pays homage to both. My next project is to tackle the kind of internal decoration at which Mackintosh excelled. But who knows when or in what form I will finally be able to achieve anything that comes close.

OPPOSITE
Museum of Modern Art.
Isozaki.
Photograph: Yukio Futagawa

Hayaski House 1976–7.
Living room by Arata Isozaki.
Photograph: Yukio Futagawa

East facade, Glasgow School of Art:
'flat abstract composition'.
Photograph: Glasgow School of Art

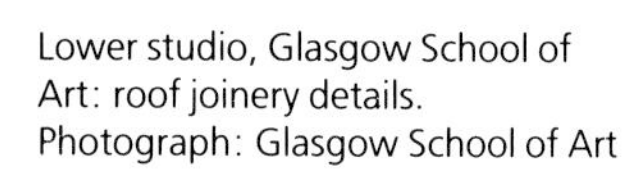

Lower studio, Glasgow School of
Art: roof joinery details.
Photograph: Glasgow School of Art

POSTSCRIPT RICHARD MURPHY

My involvement with the Contemporary Visions Exhibition dates from five months before the show was launched. Isi Metzstein introduced me to Murray Grigor, billing me as some sort of 'Mr Fixit'. The idea was strong, for once the money (courtesy of the Glasgow District Council and Bishop and Robertson Chalmers) was in place; the only problem was that only one of the invited architects had confirmed his participation. My rôle was to firm up the list, cajole designs out of the miscellaneous maestri and then organize with a brilliant team of Mackintosh School students the construction of the as yet to be imagined homages.

Architects already approached were many and various and generally chosen from both a geographical and ideological scatter. It was more by luck than by design, however, that we assembled the final team – with strong English, European, American and Oriental representation (but curiously no Scots). Ideologically we ranged from the more outrageous post-modernism of Tigerman and the studied European anti-modernism of Krier on the one hand, to the Team X veteran of modernism van Eyck with his two lieutenants: the romantic English modernist Cullinan and the Viennese Hans Hollein. Absent from the symposium, but very present in the exhibition itself, was the Japanese architect Arata Isozaki – an early admirer of Mackintosh and a modernist searching for a way of bridging Japanese and Western cultures.

The installations together with the symposium and the interviews contained in this book provoke and inform. They establish without doubt Mackintosh's remarkable influence on many of today's great architects – an influence encountered when those architects were searching early in their careers and at a time when Mackintosh found little favour in his own land.

That Mackintosh provoked such heated discussions and contrary interpretations is perhaps proof itself of the clarity of the issues raised through the medium of his own work. Issues of architectural form and coherence, symmetry and composition, plan making and place making, generality and detail, inside and outside, order and anarchy, authority and hierarchy. This is the stuff of architecture and it is no surprise that our invited architects immediately got to grips with these issues. As so often, it is the practising architect who is able to interpret the real significance of a work like the School of Art and rescue it from the all too familiar side-shows of the art historians (Hollein told a similar story of Hoffmann's neglect in Vienna). Not that our architects shrank from placing the school in its historical and social contexts: indeed the division of opinion over whether it was essentially nineteenth century (Krier), incapable of grappling with the twentieth century (Tigerman) or the first great modernist building (van Eyck) was one of the greatest unresolved questions of the symposium. Perhaps more interesting than where Mackintosh came from (Scottish vernacular, the Japanese aesthetic, European free style?) is the speculation of how he might have developed in the 1930s and beyond. Such great European contemporaries as Asplund and Hoffmann while changing their language clearly demonstrated a coherent development of thought; we can only speculate how Mackintosh would have risen to the challenge of those decades – a speculation fuelled by van Eyck, Hollein and Cullinan and their assertion of his essentially modernist credentials but dampened by the scepticism of Krier and Tigerman.

Of course it is impossible to divorce criticism from the reputation of the critic. If you see architecture as a predominantly two-dimensional activity, a thing of signs and symbols, then perhaps Tigerman's epithet 'more a kind of tea shop interior designer than an architect' is understandable. Similarly, if you subscribe to a coherent non-inventive predictable language of architecture (churches look like churches, public buildings are monumental, etc.), then Krier's dismissal of Mackintosh's inventions as 'private lunacies' is a logical step. (Although, as Andy MacMillan quipped at the symposium, 'it is the lunacies that the public love'.) Nevertheless, the divisions of opinion in this book have served to highlight issues from which the readers can then make up their own minds.

To Krier, for example, the front studio windows are 'monumental' and sit ill with the front entrance as a 'cottage door'. For van Eyck these same windows are big and generous – just doing their job. For Cullinan it is the whole centre bay that is the 'entrance', a balanced composition of the pavement brought up to the façade; a façade in equilibrium needs no forced Tigerman symmetry to correct it. The four elevations are dismissed by one school as disparate and unconnected while for the other they both have an independence responding to their site and yet they each, according to Cullinan and Hollein, inform the other. Bits of the front appear on the back and vice versa. For Krier, the library is 'a bit of a mess design-wise', with little relationship between inside and outside; for Hollein it is confirmation that Mackintosh understood about the psychology of space – about 'how books can engulf you in study'.

Perhaps the most intriguing analysis, however, is the discussion about the plan – the disposition of the bits of the school and the concomitant social organization. Here there were three interpretations. Krier and Tigerman and, unusually, Cullinan too saw nothing revolutionary about it: a standard single loaded corridor, but for Cullinan and Hollein the magic is in the place making; a creator of 'shifting experiences' (Hollein) as one circulates; making a corridor like a gallery or a studio like a living room so that each space has, for Cullinan, a multiplicity of interpretations. Van Eyck, however, made a great play of the plan – the world's first 'non-hierarchical building, mutilateral in spirit; anti Beaux Arts and anarchic'. Using the familiar analogy of 'building as small city', he described the corridors having rooms accessed equally with no implied hierarchy like a street with a collection of great and humble buildings. Most telling is the position of the director. Given prominence on the elevation and sitting centrally in the plan he is, none the less, by no means 'central' to the experience of those working in the building. A hierarchical plan would have placed in him a position which communicates authority; in the Art School we can read his rôle as leader of the team. In this sense we can understand how van Eyck stated that Mackintosh knew what the 'pulse of an Art School is all about'; a joint endeavour where the authority of staff over student is blurred, if not reversed, by the experience of a common creative quest.

These issues of formal composition, organization of spaces, response to site and social organization, etc., are what the symposium participants referred to as the conflicts within any building programme. But expression and then resolution of such conflicts are the stuff of all art. As Hollein pointed out, great works of painting, music and literature are inevitably public displays of private artistic conflicts; so why not architecture also? No matter how one interprets Mackintosh's response, it must be obvious to all that his buildings continue to provoke speculation over the very basic issues with which all architects have to deal.